W9-AOG-723

Reflections of
JESSE STUART

Books by Dick Perry

RAYMOND AND ME THAT SUMMER

THE ROUNDHOUSE, PARADISE, AND MR. PICKERING

WAS YOU EVER IN ZINZINNATI?

ONE WAY TO WRITE YOUR NOVEL

OHIO, PERSONAL PORTRAIT OF THE 17TH STATE

MORE THAN JUST A SOUND

REFLECTIONS OF JESSE STUART

Plays by Dick Perry

GO FROM ME

THE BRIEFCASE BOHEMIAN OF THE 7:54

FOREVER THE WILD, SWEET VOICE OF LOVERS

THERE'LL NEVER BE ANOTHER BONGO

WHO'LL TEACH MY BABY RAZOR-BLADES?

WHAT IT WAS, WAS OXFORD?

REFLECTIONS OF

JESSE STUART

On a Land of Many Moods

BY DICK PERRY

McGraw-Hill Book Company

NEW YORK   ST. LOUIS   SAN FRANCISCO

DÜSSELDORF   LONDON   MEXICO

SYDNEY   TORONTO

CARL A. RUDISILL LIBRARY
LENOIR RHYNE COLLEGE

818.5209
P42r
8 1935
Jan.1973

Copyright © 1971 by Dick Perry.

*All rights reserved. Printed in the United States of America.
No part of this publication may be reproduced, stored in a
retrieval system, or transmitted, in any form or by any
means, electronic, mechanical, photocopying, recording, or
otherwise, without the prior written permission of the publisher.*

Library of Congress Catalog Card Number: 77-159322

07-049450-9

First Edition

DESIGNED AT THE INKWELL STUDIO

For the ladies in our lives:
DEANE, JEAN, JANE,
and ANN

FOREWORD

I WILL tell you how this book was conceived, how and in what way it grew to fulfillment and acceptance. The Irish spawned it and the city of Cincinnati was its nest.

Georgia Glynn is all Irish—go to Ireland and visit the Irish and return to Georgia Glynn and see if she isn't more Irish than the Irish. Now, Georgia Glynn is a Cincinnatian and she used to sell books at one of the large department stores. When I went to Cincinnati to sign books for Georgia Glynn, customers were lined up. Once there were double lines ever-inching toward me! This was glory for this author.

Soft-spoken Georgia Glynn loved certain books. She loved the feel of a new book. And how she could sell them! Now I'm not sure she *should* have sold books, because soft-spoken, friendly, lovely Georgia Glynn had another special talent (no wonder there are politicians among the Irish) that of putting a writer she selected on a given subject. She chose that subject. Big publishers in the East (New York City, mostly) grabbed at her ideas and published these books! And why not? Some of them have sold 50,000—even 100,000—copies!

Georgia Glynn got to know me and I got to know her through my books and I was fond of her. But Georgia was having an Irish dream about me. She didn't think people knew me. Well, I knew I liked people and had never had too many run-ins with them, even with all the educational improvements I'd tried to make, and I'd not hidden many things about myself from people. I was really close, so I thought, in my associations with people.

"Now, Jesse, I know there have been scholarly books about you," she said. "But what about the man in the street? How well do your neighbors actually know you?"

There had been four scholarly hardback books written about me and one scholarly paperback about the humor in my work.

"Now, I've got the right man to do this book," she said. "He is Dick Perry (born in Cincinnati), who lives in Oxford, Ohio. And I've got the publisher."

Look what Georgia Glynn could have done in the publishing world! Should she have sold books, or should she have been a literary agent or worked with a publishing house?

When I met Dick Perry we were a little stand-offish at first. As two writers and we looked each other over—put out our sensitive tentacles to get some feeling. Here was a very shy man over six feet wearing a neat, well-trimmed beard. Here was I, clean-shaven, six feet, with a crew haircut. Here were an Ohioan and a Kentuckian trying to get together for a writer to write about a writer. In many ways we were so opposite. But the longer we talked the warmer our conversations grew. Still, somehow, I was dubious. Once I said to my wife, Naomi: "He'll never do this proposed book."

But Dick Perry came to an inn in Ohio, not far from here. He made this his home while he was here. His nights belonged to him. The days belonged jointly to us. All writers work differently. And, I thought, Dick Perry worked as differently as any writer I had ever known. I didn't know he was working at all. I knew he was great on taping everything. Once in a while here in the house, or while riding in my VW over the farm (and there are miles of roads on this farm), I'd let something slip that I didn't think should be on tape. And I'd say, "Delete that last remark," and he'd answer: "Don't worry. I'll never hurt you or anyone. I know what to use. I'm a careful writer."

Dick Perry often spent mornings with me. Then he would leave and go other places. He visited people on the streets and in some stores in Greenup, which is our hometown of about 1500. He traveled over country roads and talked to people who knew or who had heard of me. He visited Bud and Faye Adams, who live on and operate this farm. And before he came here, he undoubtedly had made a survey of my books, for he asked to visit certain places. One was the Plum Grove Cemetery. But I had not dreamed he had his book outlined and that he was filling in by asking me certain pointed and non-pointed questions, which I always answered.

As we stayed here at home or rode about we picked up other subjects for discussion. One was a former editor, Edward Kuhn, who had worked with both of us. We two writers here reviewed a young editor and publisher who had resigned to write his own novels. We agreed that he was a great editor with one eye on the literary product and one eye on the box office, and in agreeing, we got closer to one another—actually the Ohio River ceased to flow between when we got to talking about this editor, Edward Kuhn, Jr.

Dick asked me questions that are raised often in this country about young people today, and I told him what I thought. Basically what he was getting down to was how we

lived, and who I really was in my own community. And the
more I thought about what he was doing, the more I realized
soft-spoken, Irish dreamer, diplomat Georgia Glynn had an
original idea going here. Wouldn't I have liked to have read a
book of this type about some of my favorite writers—
Robert Frost, Carl Sandburg, Edgar Lee Masters, Scott Fitzgerald, Ernest Hemingway, yes, Mark Twain, Ralph Waldo
Emerson—written about them in their lifetimes!

Dick Perry was in this area about eight days. If he ever
took a note on paper I never saw him. But I can't recall a
time when we were together that he didn't have his tape
going. I'd never been receptive before to tapes or any kind of
recordings either. But when Dick said: "I guess this winds it
up," I was sorry to see him go.

We said our warm farewells and he drove his station
wagon down the valley.

Days, weeks, months passed. Then, Naomi and I visited
Oxford, Ohio, where I spoke at Miami University. Oxford,
Ohio, is a beautiful city with two excellent institutions of
higher learning and over 15,000 people, yet I can send a letter
to Dick Perry just simply to Oxford without a street ad-
dress and he gets it. So he must be well-known in his home
town. He attended my lecture there. Later that evening we
visited his home, met his family, his tall wife Jean, his two tall
teen-age sons and daughter, and several of his friends. He
didn't tell me, and I didn't ask him, if he had done anything
on the book he'd planned to write about me. We enjoyed the
Dick Perry family and their friends.

Later we met Dick and Jean Perry under entirely different
circumstances. We were all invited by Mr. and Mrs. Francis
Dale to the press booth at Riverfront Stadium, Cincinnati,

Ohio, to see a professional football game, Bengals versus Steelers (this was Naomi's and my first time to see a professional football game). And who is Francis Dale? I worked for his father, principal of Portsmouth High School, a genius high school principal back in 1938–1939. I never knew a greater one. His son, Francis, was in Portsmouth High School and was outstanding among the pupils in his class. He could do anything.

Francis Dale had been promoter of Riverfront Stadium. He'd had a great hand in improving the Redlegs baseball team, and in bringing the Bengals to Cincinnati. He had been young Mr. Ohio.

While I was a guest there I watched the game but I was restless. I also watched Dick Perry, who was pacing the floor, he was restless too! I was still a writer—and I was writing a 222-line poem. I finished it before the game was over.

"What do you think of this group, the press box, and all this excitement?" Dick asked me.

"I've been around the world and I've not seen anything like this," I said. "What's on your mind? What do you think?"

"You're on my mind," he said. "I'm thinking about you and the book."

But a poem was on my mind. He was writing his book in his head. I was writing my poem with my hands. We were writers.

And we were writing among these people. In the *Cincinnati Enquirer* press box Kay and "Frank" Dale (publisher of the paper) were hosts to Brady Black, editor and vice-president of the *Enquirer*, and Mrs. Black; Senator and Mrs. Robert Taft; and the mayor of Cincinnati, Eugene Reuhl-

mann; Robert Howsam, general manager of the Cincinnati
Redlegs, whose team won the National League pennant but
lost the World Series; Mr. and Mrs. Edwin Mearns (he is
dean of the College of Law, University of Cincinnati); Dr.
William Alterneier, head of surgery, Medical College, University of Cincinnati, and his wife. We had there a lot of the
people who make Ohio run. Dick Perry carried a glass and I
carried one but we didn't drink. We were thinking and we
were writing while we should have been enjoying all this.

On January 25, 1971, we received Dick Perry's manuscript. We couldn't believe that Dick had written the book.
We agreed that he must have, for we had a Xeroxed copy of
his manuscript. But we didn't know how he'd done it. Then I
said, "Dick Perry has a very special and unusual talent," and
that is the best way I can describe him. In my lifetime, I'd
known only one other man who could work this way. He is
John Bird, former editor of *Country Gentleman* and later, articles editor of the *Saturday Evening Post*.

Naomi and I agreed to read the Dick Perry book, she first
and I second, and withhold comments until I had finished.

"Well, what did you think of it?" I asked her, when I finished the last page.

"What do you think?" she asked me.

"I am surprised what he has captured," I said.

"It's a good book right up to the last two sentences," she
said. "He said between you and him there was no more left
to say. I don't believe there was ever a time when you
couldn't talk!"

"Except when I'm asleep," I said.

We agreed to wait two days and then decide if we still
agreed on our criticism of the last page. Two days passed.

We went back to the last page in the book. We decided to leave it just as Dick Perry had written it.

Dick Perry had caught something in me I had never known. Do I talk like this? I guess I do. People had paid me good fees to hear me talk. I had talked this book. Dick Perry had filled in and edited between the lines. He had known what he was doing.

He had said he wouldn't hurt me or anyone, and he didn't. His purpose was to write a non-scholarly book. He wanted to write a book on me that would interest the man on the street.

Dick is a city man but he described my farm, and I think he really achieved what he had in mind. It is a book for elementary, secondary, and college students. It is a book for a man anywhere with an average education. And I, a writer, am amazed at the way he did it.

JESSE STUART
February 9, 1971

"If there is an agony to Spring,
and there is,
it is that Spring exists."

ONE

ARE you a teacher who writes, or a writer who teaches?"

Jesse Stuart gazed at me, rubbed his crew cut, pondered a moment, then said:

"Well, Dick, that's a good question. You know, I love both of them. I've never been asked that question before. I guess I have to do both or die. Let me put it to you like that. I love to teach. I like high school youth. I don't know why it is, but I just like 'em. I wouldn't be a good elementary teacher. My wife, Naomi Deane, is though. It's hard for me to go down into the grades. I don't think I could do it. High school is the level I like. All my life, it has been high school. I once gave a speech called 'If I Were Seventeen Again.' I just love that age. What I'm saying, Dick, is . . ."

Thus began the week-long conversation with Jesse Stuart, the Kentucky writing man. He has been studied a lot and from nearly every angle. Dissertations have been written on him. Eve Blair, Lee Pennington, Mary Washington Clarke, and Ruel Foster wrote four book-length ones. Murray State College brims with his papers, scrapbooks, correspondence, and other literary oddments. But not *all* his papers are deposited there. More are in an old smokehouse in W-Hollow in

I

the Kentucky hills where Jesse Stuart lives. Schoolchildren
have read him. So have their parents. The New York literary
circle has praised him. They called his *Man with a Bull-
tongue Plow* an outstanding American poetic work. They
gave him the same place in literature they gave Burns, Hous-
man, Masefield, Masters, and Frost. He has lectured just
about everywhere in the United States—and in many other
countries, too. Some know him as a novelist, some know him
as a poet, some know him as an educator, some know him as
a speaker, but few—hardly any, in fact—know him as a
person. They know him only as a legendary writing man.

He seems to have kin everywhere. I spent one afternoon
with him in a Cincinnati department store where he was au-
tographing books. The line moved with painful slowness because everyone—old men, young schoolteachers, high
school kids, all—felt they knew him as a friend. Most had
met him only on the printed page, but some had heard him
lecture. Others mentioned names of mutual acquaintances.
Jesse Stuart would concentrate on each person, as if they
were the only two in the room, peering at them and growing
enthusiastic when, by tracing the inner-workings of make-
shift genealogy, he discovered a thread that connected them
both. To hear Jesse Stuart and such a stranger find that each
is the other's kin is to develop the uneasy feeling that all civilization began in Greenup County, Kentucky, where he first
saw the light of day on August 8, 1907. He would look over
to me and say:

"My goodness, Dick, isn't this wonderful? I knew this
lady's father. Why, I taught him in school. He was a fine
man!"

Or, say:

"Do you realize, Dick, this man and me are second cousins on the Hilton side of the family? His father and my aunt used to . . ."

But few have had the opportunity to talk with him—and that's what this book is about: conversations with Jesse Stuart, only that and nothing more.

Jesse Stuart can be reduced, if you like quick summaries, to ordinary details. His father was a tenant farmer who couldn't read or write. He grew up in a one-room log cabin near a coal mine in the hills in back of Greenup, the slowpoke county seat of Greenup County. He started his education in a one-room, one-teacher school for grades one through eight. He farmed the hollows and the steep hillsides. He managed to get through high school in the days when a high school diploma was a luxury and a surprise. He entered Vanderbilt University with $130 in his pockets. Before that he had hitch-hiked to Lincoln Memorial University with only $29.30 in his pockets, graduating with a B average and a suitcase half-filled with themes and poems. He taught school in Greenup a year, then went to the aforementioned Vanderbilt for a year of graduate work. He came home, became superintendent of the Greenup County Schools at the age of twenty-four, and slowly evolved into the writing man he was to be. In 1934 *Man with a Bull-tongue Plow* was published, to be selected later as one of the world's 1000 best books. In 1936, he received a Guggenheim Fellowship, went to Europe for a year, came back and married Naomi Deane, had a daughter, and that pretty much is that. But is that all there is to him? Jesse Stuart is more than words on paper. He's moods and dreams and frustrations and fidgets, too.

W-Hollow, where he now lives, is where he started life.

With the sale of each poem, he bought land. Now he owns
1000 acres of the land he grew up on: some of it is hill and
some of it is hollow. He has, through the years, turned his
1000 acres into a poem filled with remembrances. This is another side of Jesse Stuart. And there's Jesse Stuart of the
world of nations in conflict and national premises that have
gone skittering. There are many Jesse Stuarts. Only through
his conversations are the other sides of him revealed.

There's the Jesse Stuart of the breakfast table that morning
in Cincinnati. He and I, along with his wife, Naomi Deane,
and my wife, Jean, and that book authority, Georgia Glynn,
sat around the hotel restaurant discussing the practical facets
of this beautiful and melancholy writing trade in which we
are both involved. Georgia Glynn was a Cincinnati department store book-buyer who had the ear—and friendship
—of publishers as well as authors.

And as writers will, we got to comparing our work sched-
ules.

"My typical working day," he said, "means I get up anywhere from six to seven-thirty. I don't get up earlier because
I like to watch the eleven o'clock news and sports before I go
to bed; and I like my seven hours sleep. I needed seven hours
sleep all my life. But when I get up in the morning, I don't always go to the desk. I always have things planned ahead.
Sometimes I'll look at letters. Sometimes I'll write a short
story. Sometimes I'll write on an article. And, you may not
believe this, but sometimes I'll paste things in my scrapbook.
I have to! Nobody else can do it. I wish I had a secretary that
could. After I've written so many days, I'll take a couple of
days off and revise. And in the afternoon, sometimes Naomi
Deane and I are liable to break out and go to some antique

store or some old bookstore or go somewhere and eat. It's always in the afternoon, though. We never go out in the morning. The mornings are for work."

"Do you write in longhand?" I said.

"Oh, I can do it either way," he said. "I have done a lot in
longhand. I always write poems in longhand."

Something bothered me.

"Do you ever find," I said, "that when you've read a book
and find a phrase you particularly like, you might use it later
in your own writing?"

He nodded.

"Yeah," he said, "and I have to watch that. One time I
used two lines in a poem and so help me, the rest of the poem
was as original as could be. The two lines had come right out
of someone else's poem. But I caught it before I sent it out.
The lines had stuck in my head and that's all there was to it.
It wasn't intentional. I don't have to do that. I have so much
to say, to write, that I don't have to take from anybody.
Other writers might stir me with what they've written,
though."

"Do you get many letters from people wanting to be writers?" I said.

He rubbed his hands together as if he were washing them.
"Oh my, yes," he said. "I get them all the time. I answered
one this week with a postcard. The letter to me was a long
one, and Naomi Deane read it and I said, 'Well, what did she
want?' Naomi Deane said she wanted me to tell how to become a writer. I said, 'Well, what would you suggest?' She
said, 'On a postcard I would tell her to go back to school!' "

"What were you looking for someone to tell you when
you were starting out?" I said.

He grinned. "I wanted somebody to tell me I was a genius, but no one ever did. Anyway, who cares? Look at the ones they call genius. A lot of the bright ones, real fine students, turned out to be elevator operators. Now the elevators are mostly automatic," he added with wonder, as if to say, where have the genius children fled?

There are other Jesse Stuarts. There is the Jesse Stuart who wrote:

> *Summer is season for the wind and sun.*
> *Summer is season for to gather food*
> *And put away before the summer ends—*
> *To store before the winter has begun.*
> *Summer is time to work, for night is coming,*
> *The grasshopper will pine, the ant will thrive,*
> *The grasshopper did dance and flit and sing*
> *Over the blackberry vine on sputtering wings.*
> *The ant did summer work that he may live*
> *Through winter's cold—and let ants work to live!*
> *And let grasshoppers dance and sing and pine*
> *And flit on summer days across the berry vine!*
> *Do summer work, for winter night is coming!*
> *One time to work—work for the night is coming!*

And there is the Jesse Stuart who stood beside me on a rail fence that marked off his hollow and, full of remembering, said:

"This land is too expensive now, Dick. If I had to start over at today's prices, I couldn't begin to buy it. I've paid seventeen dollars an acre for some of this when nobody wanted it. Now I've got some that will sell for three thousand dollars an acre. I know because I have been offered that.

But I'd be crazy to mark this land off in little building sites and sell it or sell it as a lump. Sell a seventeen-dollar acre of land for three thousand dollars and it all goes up in taxes. You're caught either way you move."

"But would you sell it at all?" I said.

Yes, we talked about a lot of things in these conversations because there are *many* Jesse Stuarts. There is Jesse Stuart of his yesterdays:

"My mother smoked," he said during one conversation, amused by the memory. "My dad smoked and chewed tobacco. My dad would take a drink of whisky, too. Loved it! My mother thought he got too much and since she was strong against it, she took to watching him. I think that influenced my life right there. She told me drinking was a waste of time and money. *Time*—there was something. My dad lived by the watch. Time, time, time. Time was the greatest thing Dad had. You had to work, for the night was coming. That was his philosophy that he passed down to me. Here was a man they called illiterate, but oh, he was smart. Look at the kids he had. Every one of us is a college graduate and we had the least of any kids in the county. Every one of us a college graduate and we all taught school. All together we've taught more than a century of school. . . ."

There is the Jesse Stuart of the world, reader of today's angry headlines. Once, sitting in the kitchen of his house with him, I sensed this anger in him. Mostly he is country-courtly. To show true anger in front of company didn't sit well with him, but I sensed it as he said:

"Power. People are using it wrong these days. Look at Julius Caesar. I was reading an article about him the other day.

E. B. White wrote it. Julius Caesar started out strong. There was a time in his life he had all the prominent women in his country making eyes at him. Oh, he was a big lover, and he was something. But then he got involved with power and how that man advanced! He was a good soldier. But he got up there and got to thinking he was a god. All the Romans got afraid of him. Unlike this country when we had Roosevelt. Nobody seemed to get afraid of Roosevelt, did they, and he was the same. But they all got afraid of Caesar and killed him."

He had drummed his fingers on the kitchen table, peered at me to see if I was a believer, too, then had gone on:

"Do you know what *my* philosophy is, Dick? It's to build and not to destroy. You build and you have to keep building. You can't turn around and start destroying. I figure there are two kinds of people in the world today: the constructionists and the destructionists. They're not Democrat or Republican or Catholic or Protestant; they're just those two categories and that's all. When the world gets to the place the destructionists outnumber the constructionists, you've the Roman Empire all over again when she vanished. Look at the airplane hijackers. Look at the problems on campus, damaging and destroying. Look at the fellows who blew up those planes in the Middle East. But I think the world is waking up to that destructive stuff. Society has to wake up to it if society wants to live. Everybody is too involved in sweetness and light. They don't want to upset people with the truth. Well, I say sweetness doesn't always bring light. You have to take a stand and get *involved*. Even if you get hurt, and oh, listen, they can hurt you out there. . . ."

There is the Jesse Stuart who wrote:

America, why don't you speak for us!
America, why don't you speak to us!
Above our beds the leaves hang tremulous
And gossip to the silver sheets of wind.
Now speak to us, for we are left behind
And you push on, America—and on.
Speak out for us—let poets rise and sing
But not of butterflies or white-moth wing;
But let them sing of earth and men of power,
And let them sing of seasons and the flower—
To hell with singers' sentimental songs,
Let them go sing for men where they belong.
Give us a singer that will sing for us—
The truth of us—then listen to his song
For we must sleep—and our sleep shall be long!

There is the Jesse Stuart, also, of the classroom: the teaching man.

"I taught remedials," he said one time in his living room. "I wish I had kept a record of my remedial students. I missed a great book there. They did more than the good students did. I had them in English. I had one that was always sleeping in class, so one day the rest of the class and I stood around and threw the *Portsmouth Times* at him to wake him up. Well, he sure woke up fast and do you know what he said? He said, 'Mr. Stuart, I thought I was in the clouds and that a flock of geese had hit me.' Beautiful, beautiful . . . But do you know what is really beautiful? He went on to Ohio State University where he made the dean's list—and I had him in a remedial class!"

So many memories flowed from Jesse Stuart, the teacher.

Another time while we strolled the meadow high atop a W-Hollow ridge he said:

"I gave a talk a little while ago in a high school that has nearly two thousand students. They caught a lad there stealing and called the police. You know where they sent him? To the reform school. That wasn't my way when *I* was teaching. I had a mission. I was out to save the children. One of my remedial students one time pulled a switchblade knife in my classroom, getting ready to stick another boy with it, but I just raised up, hit him, and laid him out cold. We weren't supposed to touch students but I sure did. We locked the door so the principal couldn't see, we got some smelling salts, and we brought him around. When he came to, he thanked me. He came right out and said, 'Thank you, Mr. Stuart.' Why? He had come from reform school and they had put him in my room as a remedial. If I had sent him to the principal's office he would have been sent back to reform school. But he thanked me and never got into another thing."

"Whatever became of him?" I said.

Jesse Stuart looked at the sky. He seemed remotely angry about something.

"He was killed in World War Two," said the teacher. "He was killed fighting for his country."

Jesse Stuart has many stories and, like this one, some of them can break your heart.

As we stood in the meadow that day atop the ridge, he said:

"We didn't have a textbook in that class. The only textbook I ever used was the *Portsmouth Times*. We analyzed sentences from it, diagramed, and wrote. I let them memorize any poems they wanted; some memorized some pretty good poems, too. The principal didn't agree with the way I was teaching them when he found out about it. So he came in the room one day, put a big sentence on the blackboard, and diagramed it himself. He was a fine fellow and a real scholar. I said, 'You're just wonderful. I couldn't have diagramed that sentence myself.' I told him that right in front of the students. I said, 'We're not that far along yet.' He was wise, like I said. He understood and got out. He left me alone with my remedial students."

"Are there remedial students, or are there just teachers who cause the students to make a mess of learning?" I said.

"There *are* remedial students," he said. "Poorly trained ones. And there are poorly trained teachers. I know because I've seen 'em. Not too many, but they are there."

"Does that bother you?" I said.

"My goodness, yes," he said. "Lives are at stake in the classroom. Entire futures. But I've seen some good teachers, awfully good ones. Portsmouth had 'em. They were high-level. The students I had were the outcasts and the downtrodden, though. There was one boy in my class who showed me things he had written. I said, 'Did you really write these poems?' He said, 'Yes, Mr. Stuart. They're mine.' I showed his poems to the principal. He couldn't believe such good could come from one of my remedials. 'He couldn't have written them,' the principal said. We checked the boy's IQ. He was in the genius bracket!"

In another conversation, Jesse Stuart said:

"I have this feeling when I'm in a classroom, teaching. I'm the father of everybody there. With me, they're going to get a fair deal. I'm going to protect the girls and help the boys. I'm going to teach them and give them things in life that will help them. No one should ever teach school just to get through the day. The day is too important. Teaching is of the heart as well as of the mind. Goodness knows, these pupils need all the character-building they can get, because once they leave school, a lot of it washes away anyway. You have to love to teach. It's as simple as that. Teaching is not just a way to get through another day. . . ."

Then, there is the puzzled Jesse Stuart. One day, sorting through his mail, he looked up and said to me:

"If I had a son, I'd name him Bruce. That's a name nobody can corrupt. Look at this."

He showed me a letter addressed to "Jessie Stuart."

"It's *Jesse* Stuart," he said, "and this here is from a good friend of mine."

"And the name *Stuart?*" I said.

"They spell it every way in the book," he sighed. "It's a wonder my mail ever gets through at all."

He went back to his mail—and found three more misspellings. He said no more on the subject. He just looked at the envelopes and shrugged. Even a poet can't fight city hall.

The farmer-turned-teacher-turned-poet is a big-boned man who stands over six feet tall, presenting the appearance of a gentle bear that wouldn't hurt a flea. He has, as suggested, a crew cut. He has the habit of peering at you, concentrating completely, shutting out the diversions of the world. He is a nervous man, full of fidgets. You can sense the power of him as you can sense the power of a great steam locomotive panting on a siding waiting for the highball. A heart attack has slowed him a little but you sense the power still waits. If need be, I had the feeling, he could still outwrestle the village bully. He speaks softly, is courteous almost to a fault, but words pour out of him—torrents of words shaped into paragraphs—like a mountain stream running out with winter snow. He is young. I mean this. He is young. His youth shows in his eyes, his enthusiasm, and his sense of wonder. He still marvels over things most of us have long since taken for granted: windy skies, mended fences, mountain shacks, starry nights, pine trees, pastures, katydids, whippoorwills, and the nighthawk's scream.

And those unwashed children we have labeled *hippies*. In one conversation, he said:

"A hippie colony started out around here, right up there close to Huntington. They rented an old house and ran around in it naked. One young man in the colony was the one they tried in California: Manson. His father and mother were from these parts. You can't pull that kind of stuff around here, I mean, going out like they do, living that way, and pillaging the countryside. On the other hand, this country around here is fair. One time a bunch of their musicians came in and slept on the ground and all, but nobody bothered them. That's because they weren't going to stay on. Have you seen many hippies in Ashland, Dick? Or in Huntington? You might see a few there because of Marshall College and maybe a few in Ashland because it's got a University of Kentucky center, but we don't have many. Ohio State University has 'em. So has Ohio University in Athens. I think that sort cheapens education. They want everything handed to them. The schools are at fault some, too. They take in anybody and pass out credits like candy. Why, my goodness, there's one boy I taught in high school who went on and got his master's degree. How he did that I'll never know. He couldn't read worth a lick."

These, then, are conversations with Jesse Stuart. That's all this book is. It covers a week spent talking with this Kentucky writing man. Sometimes we talked in his home. Sometimes we went places, such as to the Plum Grove Cemetery, and all about the meadows of his 1000-acre farm. This is one writing man talking to another. Sometimes we talked about the writing profession itself and sometimes about the way the world is. Mostly, though, I listened.

Talking with Jesse Stuart is the easiest job in the world. You don't have to say much. You listen a lot and you don't want to say anything, either, because you don't want to halt the flow. So in this book, you can sit around with me, listening. Here you will see sides of the writer he has not had time to put into words before. Or, on the other hand, you may prick up your ears and hear an old story—one you've read—retold, or learn how the writing of it came about. You'll hear what his dad thought of versifying. His dad did not exactly get excited about the fact his son could rhyme words.

"He never went for writing," Jesse Stuart told me. "He never understood it. He went for schoolteaching. To him a schoolteacher was the highest form of person. The greatest day in his life was when I was sworn in as county school superintendent. He laid off that day from the railroad section crew, dressed up in a blue serge suit, a big black hat, wearing a tie and a pale blue faded workshirt to come see the swearing-in."

"But when he saw you making money as a poet?"

"I never made much money as a poet," Jesse Stuart said.

We'll go into that, too: the economics of a poet in this day and age.

Jesse Stuart covered the full range during the conversations. One afternoon, when we were talking about moonshine, he said, "You know, Dick, that Kentucky distills ninety percent of the world's bourbon, but we have to go to Ohio around here to get liquor? Lawrence County over the river has the second busiest state liquor package store in Ohio. The first, I think, is in Cleveland. But Ironton's number two. The state liquor stores in West Virginia get some business from us, but most around here cross over to Ironton. Do you know what the people in Ashland call the Ironton store? They call it the 'People's Store'! All who drink in Ashland buy over there. It's the busiest liquor store. It has about ten men working in it. That's how busy it is!"

Fair warning: I am fond of this Kentucky writing man. If you seek, via these pages, ugliness, seek elsewhere. I have put down the conversations as fairly and as accurately as I could. They were all recorded on tape. The tapes are still around my study somewhere. I can, via the magic of modern machinery, bring back any afternoon with Jesse Stuart, hear his voice again, hear the other sounds—the tickings of a clock or the cry of the cricket—and it all comes back. I have, with a writer's reason, edited his conversations here and there. I edited not to hide something from you but to organize us better. I am afraid that in conversation there are times Jesse Stuart and I, as everyone does, rambled. There was so much to say and so little time to say it. The many clocks in his living room, all ticking gently, reminded us that we could not keep talking forever.

"Sooner or later," said Jesse Stuart one afternoon, "I guess we have to stop so you can get this all down somehow on paper."

But we kept delaying the ending of this conversation—
these conversations. He was fond of talking to me. For that
I am grateful. I was fond of listening. It was a pleasant week
of non-stop talk. We covered, it seemed, everything. Yet we
never seemed to run out.

For instance, once I asked him, "Was there ever a moment
your family considered giving up life as tenant farmers and
moving to a city?"

"They never wanted the city," he said swiftly. He had to
impress me with this important and beautiful fact. "They
wanted rural. Once they talked about a farm in Ohio, but
Dad wouldn't leave. Then once they talked about a farm in
Illinois. Somebody had told my dad about the black soil there,
and anyway, he wanted to go out into a Republican county.
But he never went places much."

I thought of the steep hillsides Jesse Stuart and his dad had
farmed.

"But somewhere along the line," I said, "he might have
moved to Illinois. It would have been easier to farm there
than here."

Jesse Stuart agreed. "It would have been easier to farm," he
said, "but my dad didn't know about it. He had never been
there himself. He'd only heard about how it was. Somebody
had told him the soil was black as a black hat. And by golly,
it was! The first time I ever went to Chicago, I rode a train
across Illinois. I was going to California and I was riding
across northern Illinois and I called the porter and said,
'What's that on the ground out there?' He said, 'My boy,
that's the way God made it. That's *black* soil. . . .' See, the
glacier had brought it down. What a land, Dick! That land,

without fertilizer or anything, would bring one hundred bushels an acre. *That's* farm land. Oh, if we had had some of that, if the Stuarts had had some of that, what would have happened...."

The idea obsessed him.

The idea of our country obsesses him, too. He feels youth is frittering the dream away, and he becomes troubled. We were on this subject one morning. I was pointing out that the children were of a different moment in time. Their sense of history was not ours. They had no Pearl Harbor to anger them. They had been born in the fifties, mostly, and had come of age with even the Korean War behind them.

He accepted this but it saddened him.

"They ought to know a little history," he said. "They ought to know a little blood was shed to make this country what it is. They ought to be conscious of these things. I read a 'letter to the editor' in a newspaper the other day. It said there's no chance for this country. Well, if that's the way the letter-writer feels, let him go somewhere else. Let him go to Russia. These women who get up and make speeches about liberation here—if they want freedom, let them go to Russia where the women aren't free. Let them all get out of here and go see where freedom ends. It ends mostly at our borders, Dick. Here is where freedom is. But they don't know. I think travel would be the best thing for some of these young people. Their fathers are giving them plenty of money. Let them take it and go see how other people live. Let them see the people in Pakistan. In India. In Korea. I've seen 'em and I know. Free China over there isn't as big as West Virginia but it's as mountainous—and it's got forty million people all saying thank you to Uncle Sam. Let the young people go out and hear that!"

For Jesse Stuart is the man who said:

I've met you many times before, Defeat.
Not every time we fought you blacked my eyes,
For many times I've staggered to my feet
And hit you hard enough to break your ribs.
You know, Defeat, I whipped you at the plow.
I fought you at hot furnaces of steel.
You whipped me at the circus, made a show of me—
Of me for men to see—and now I feel
That when we meet again, one man must kill.

Come, if you please.
Let us go visit a poet who has made a poem of the land.

TWO

WE were standing in the first living room—the Jesse Stuart home has two—and Jesse Stuart was talking about the huge wooden table on which his wife was sorting pages of a manuscript.

"My mother used to iron on that table," Jesse Stuart was saying. "She took some of the leaves out and it just didn't work right for her so she just took a hatchet and some big nails—and there it sits. You couldn't move that table after my mother fixed it!"

The Stuart home in the hollow began its life years before when the poet as a boy had lived there with his parents. The house was smaller then, a dinky cabin. Later it became a cowshed. After Jesse Stuart married, they cleaned it up again—and he's been there ever since.

The place grew as the writing man's stature grew. When Jesse and Naomi Deane first set up housekeeping, they lived in the two-room lean-to that had been the home of his father as well as his grandparents. Now it is a nine-room house. The first living room, which you enter from the outside, has a brick fireplace. Go one way and you head to the dining room and on to the kitchen. Turn left and you head through Jesse

Stuart's study into another living room, beyond which is the
master bedroom done with Lincoln-period mahogany furniture. Every room is warm and comfortable and feels "lived-
in." There are two other bedrooms: one, off the first living
room, belonged to their daughter and upstairs, around a steep
curve, is another bedroom in the loft.

Clocks are everywhere, old-fashioned clocks with swinging
pendulums, ticking, chiming, in every room. Some are man-
sized grandfather clocks; others are antique mantel-sized
beauties. No reasons for them save that the Stuarts like the
sound of their muted tickings. And in every room, books
abound.

"How many books do you think are in the house?" I
asked.

"Maybe ten thousand," said Jesse Stuart.

"I think books make beautiful furniture," I said.

The poet agreed. "I do, too," he said, "and I just love
them—*period*."

Naomi Deane looked up from her sorting.

"Why don't you boys go out for a while," she said.
"Lunch isn't ready yet. I put the air conditioner on and it's
making my bread rise differently."

Jesse Stuart and I wandered through the kitchen to the
back yard. From under a shed a raccoon peered out at us,
worried. The writer told me about the animal.

"She doesn't do any digging," he said. "Whatever digging
she has to do, she's already done. That's where she lives.
Only sometimes she lives down here, under the house. She
goes down by the pipe. There's no basement under the house,
but under there is her home. See those walnut trees yonder?
My mother set those out and she set out those over there, too.

I set the dogwoods. I set the chestnut trees over there on the hill. And I set this pine right here. . . . "

Behind the house, the back yard went up at a steep slant to the top of the ridge hidden by the trees. The sun of September warmed us as we stood, gaping about.

"I like the silence of this place," I said. "Can you hear train whistles or riverboats back here in the hollow?"

"No," said Jesse Stuart. "But we can sure hear the planes going over. Did you ever see such timber, Dick? We've enough timber in this back yard to build another house. Looky at that pine tree yonder through there. Squirrels build their nests in it and have their young. And in the same tree is a dove's nest. Do you know who digs around the yard this way? Our friends, the polecats. They come in and take the grubs out of the ground. They're valuable."

He gazed about in contentment. He pointed to a place on the hillside. He said without rancor:

"Up there, right up there, is where I had my first heart attack. Right up there on that bank."

He looked back at the house, though, as if to change his train of thought.

"We made this house," he said with pride. "It's my wife's house. You ought to have seen at the beginning what it was when we came here."

"If you had it to do over again," I said, "would you go after the same kind of place?"

"My goodness, yes," he said. "We'd go after exactly the same kind. What I mean is, we just *live* this way. That's another thing, though. If we didn't hold firm, they'd turn our home into a showplace. You've been around and seen how everybody wants to come to the house. . . . "

Yes, I had seen. In some way, it had broken my heart. I knew he loved visitors but these days too many visitors exhausted him. I had seen the Stuarts inside their beautiful home, curtains drawn, door shut, as if they had gone somewhere else. I had seen them sitting in their well-appointed prison, worrying at the sound of any car that came up the hollow road, hiding as the raccoon hides, loving people, needing people, but afraid of the exhaustion that people, without meaning to, can cause. Jesse Stuart and his wife lead full—and sometimes lonely—lives in the silent hollow. But this is the price of fame. This is what poetry and love are all about.

"Naomi Deane has done the house," Jesse Stuart was saying. "She loves that house, Dick. So we just kept adding rooms to it and there it sits. We're happy here. We hardly ever go out calling. We entertain here and when we cook, we put on a couple filets. I don't get as expensive food other places when I go out and buy it as I get right here at home."

"You're a kind of legend, aren't you?" I said.

We settled on a bench behind the house. He rubbed his jaw and peered at me, bemused.

"I can't any more believe that than if I got up and stood on my head," he said. "But people believe it. They tell me it is true, that I *am* legendary." He seemed bewildered by the classification. "It's hard for me to believe it, though. But that's the way they treat me. Gosh, Dick, it gets harder and harder for me to go lecturing because you should see the way the people do. They keep wanting me to go into their homes. They keep wanting to entertain me. To them I am a legend but I'm not to me. Now some of them have found out that I take a little Scotch in the evening. I used to be narrow on that. I was really narrow on that. I don't want to go into it, but I was narrow on drinking. I was wrong, though. Now I take a drink as medicine and it helps me. So now they bring me bottles of Scotch—old friends and students do—because they know I'll take a drink. They come in here, bringing the best. But as for being a legend . . ."

He made a helpless motion with his hands.

"To them," I said, "the legend is a reality."

He nodded.

"I suppose," he said, not liking the subject much. "Another thing, Dick, is when strangers come here. They always want to take something from the place, a piece of wood off it or something. They want old barn planks to make picture frames out of. They'll get it, too, because I'll go out and help them find something they're after."

"They want something—anything—as a souvenir of W-Hollow?" I said.

"Yep, just so it's from this farm," he said. "Then, they want me to *verify* that what they got *is* from the farm. They want me to authenticate it with a piece of paper. I've done that for 'em, too. But I don't understand it. They're welcome to the old wood. It would rot anyway. Some of it, I mean, some of it in the barn."

"Aren't you afraid that someday somebody's going to set up a tourist stand, selling concessions and Jesse Stuart souvenirs?" I said.

He pondered that.

"Well," he said finally, "it might happen after I'm gone and after Naomi Deane is gone, but we wouldn't have that now. I wouldn't let it happen and neither would she. I would be kind of embarrassed. But it's going on, maybe, in Edgar

Lee Masters country out there in Illinois. Masters wouldn't have wanted it either, but how do you stop them? Masters wouldn't have understood it, people making money off his memory, because when he was living, look at the hard time he had getting together the price of a meal. He was hungry lots of times."

"I understand," I said, "a James Thurber shopping center is going up in Columbus, Ohio."

He shrugged. The shrug said the world was too much for writers.

We watched as a station wagon loaded with children moved slowly up the hollow road. In front of the house, it paused, the driver made a Y, turned, and there went the car back out of the hollow again.

"They're always coming back here," Jesse Stuart said. "Sometimes they stop in and many is the Sunday we'll have a house full of strangers. But they're all fine people. They're all age levels, too, like that car there."

"When you appear on local television," I said, "like on the Bob Braun program over WLW-Television, is your home inundated after that for a while?"

He nodded.

"That Bob Braun," he said, "does a wonderful job. I just wish we could get WLWT this far up the river. We're about twenty miles short of pulling them in good. His program reaches Portsmouth, but it doesn't reach this far without giving out. But his is a marvelous program for these people here. If he could reach up to Ashland and Huntington I just know he would have an awful good following. I like that fellow."

"Do you watch television much?" I said.

He shook his head.

"No," he said. "I'm a radio man myself. I'll listen to the radio, especially FM programs. I use good FM music while I work. But when the news comes on, I'll cut it off because the news bothers me. All that talking, I mean. I'll cut it off and wait for the music to come back. I can work to music but I can't work to talking. I can't do it."

"You don't like most of television?"

"It has ruined the country in some ways," he said. "There's a great shift on in the way people think. Look at how television has shown the police. On television, the police were always coming into a room, beating people in the stomach, and look at the name the police have now."

"You have appeared on educational television, haven't you?" I said.

"Yep," he said. "I have. It's a great medium, Dick. I forget who made the comment but it was sure a profound one that it's a great medium but it's not for little boys to play with. Look what television can do. It can change wars. It can change *anything!* I love the sports it brings me, but I think people have run television into the ground. It has changed the children who watch it, hasn't it? What do you think a child thinks when he sees these robbings and murders and when he sees the policeman always put in a bad light? Also, it hangs 'em up because in real life robberies and murders aren't solved in a half hour the way they are on television. You can't solve them like that, that fast. Nobody can. Who writes these things anyway? How much experience have the writers had in *anything?* They go to the sensational to sell their wares. High sensationalism. Who grades them on what they write? The trouble is, it's all centered in New York and Hollywood where the people have the least morals and the least horse sense of anybody around."

We watched a corn bird dart among the trees.

"We had less entertainment in my day," he was saying. "I remember when I was a high school senior and walked through the little town of Greenup. My dad's second cousin said, 'Come over here, Jesse, and listen to this.' He was sitting at a table and had earphones on. I went over, put the earphones on, and heard KDKA. First time I ever heard anything like that in my life! He said to me, 'Boy, this thing will change the world. You wait and see.' And my goodness, it did, didn't it? I mean, radio. Radio became our great entertainment. Now there's radio *and* television and look at what we've got. Still, some of those sports broadcasts are out of this world.

"Ball games interest me. Baseball is good, clean competition. I like anything where you have to battle for something. I *like* competition. Yet, I've met educators who say now they're knocking competition. Why? In high school, I always chose someone to compete against and that would make a better student of me. And I'd get them competing, too; we'd both be better for it. When I taught, I'd get the girls to compete with the boys and the boys to compete with the girls, all with each other."

"Some students say the trouble with the world today is the result of competition instead of love," I said.

He jumped on that quick as a cat.

"I disagree with the kids on that," he said. "They can have *both:* the love of competition and the love of doing it to improve themselves. I have taught kids to love one another when I was teaching. But I taught competition, too. Competition is what has made the world. It's what has made this country. It's dangerous, I'll admit, but when people don't compete, they're dead. Why, my goodness, competition is the spice of life. I can show you how even at restaurants. The old ones around here just kept moseying along until some new ones came in to compete. Now this area has great restaurants because there's great competition among them."

"But," I said, "is the eagerness to compete dying in this country?"

"I sure hope it doesn't," Jesse Stuart said, rubbing his crew cut. "If competition goes, we're all goners, too. But I don't think it's going. Look at that ball player up in Cincinnati, Pete Rose. When he plays that game, he gets right in there and argues and competes. I saw him doing it the other night on television during a game. Television that's live doesn't lie, you know. You see even some things on television that the umpires miss. When a ball hits the line, whether it's fair or foul, the camera is watching too, so the umpire had better call it right. The other night an umpire called a foul ball on Cincinnati that was no more a foul ball than the moon is. Pete Rose went out to argue it. Why, I thought for a minute they were going to throw him out of the game. If all the television viewers that were watching that game would have called in, we could have verified that Pete Rose was right and the umpire was wrong. Cincinnati hit it out there fair but they counted it foul. Two men had scored on it but they had to go back. But that Pete Rose is sure something. Is he a big fellow standing next to you, Dick?"

"Not too tall," I said.

This saddened the poet. Huge men like to presume their heroes are Paul Bunyans, too.

"Well," said Jesse Stuart, trying to salvage something, "he *looks* big."

"They wouldn't let him play basketball too much in high school," I said, "Because of his height."

"He's not a runt now," the poet exclaimed. "He got a home run when the Reds were playing the Padres the last game here. He really untied one that made the score four to three. Derned if they didn't come back in the ninth inning with two runs to beat the Reds. Those Padres! And everywhere else, they *lose!* They're the low ones in the Western Division of the National League." He got a look in his eye. "I'd just love to see a game of the World Series," he said.

"Have you been to see the Reds play in the new stadium?" I said.

"Yes," he said. He didn't seem happy about it. "We specified what seats we wanted and they put us right in back of the score board. Had to climb too high. I climbed up to the last row—and there was only one tier of seats above us. You couldn't even tell where the ball was going when it got hit."

"Is the stadium too big, perhaps?" I said.

"No, oh no," he said quickly. "It's just that I always like to sit behind and see the ball go out in front of me. I can usually judge about where she'll be hit. Anyway, we sat up there and watched the Redlegs and they won, so we enjoyed it. Did you know they lost last night, though?"

"I hope they win the Western Division title," I said.

"They've got it cinched," the poet assured me. "They sure
have. . . ."

Later, when autumn was on the land, Jesse Stuart and I
would be in Riverfront Stadium in Cincinnati and see the
Bengals play. We would be sitting beside *Enquirer* publisher
Francis Dale, friend of Jesse Stuart and one of the prime
movers in getting the stadium itself built. We would be in the
glass-enclosed box in the most comfortable seats imaginable,
in a world that would awe both of us. The box was a warm,
private living room, a buffet was spread for our nibbling pleasure, the bar was stocked, and a bartender and a waiter were
in attendance. Jesse Stuart, farmer-poet, would later write of
it:

> *Colossal Riverfront's grandeur!*
> *Architecture akin to Greece and Rome,*
> *Riverfront, Bengals, and the Redlegs' home.*
> *With lights aglow:*
>   *We watch the game below,*
> *Down on that artificial April green,*
> *Carpet for Bengals and the Red Machine!*
> *Upend and bend, flip in the air, and fall!*
> *Go, Bengals, go!*
>   *Go, America, go!*
> *This is the finest hour,*
>   *To show your power,*
> *The power of man-giants, win, lose or draw!*
> *Within this Stadium is the Bengal claw.*
> *Olympic in Pindar's beloved Greece*
> *Or anything they ever had in Rome*

Will not surpass Riverfront Stadium,
The Red Legs, Bengals home,
Circular wall with tier on tier around,
Spectators looking out, over and down!
Go, Bengals, go!
Go, Bengals, go!
Go, Bengals, go!
What about two wins, three wins, four wins in a row!

But that would be later. Meanwhile, Jesse Stuart and I stood in his back yard, talking sports. We were discussing favorite baseball players.

"Mine," I said, "was Ernie Lombardi." He used to catch for the Reds.

"My hero was Babe Ruth," said Jesse Stuart. "He was great. He's never been equaled. And I'm tickled to death about Johnny Bench. They worship him around Greenup County. I don't think you can find anybody around here that's not a Redleg fan. Why, these people back in the hills —the grandmothers and the great grandmothers—sit up till two in the morning listening to a Redleg game broadcast. That's the truth! J. T. Lawson stopped me the other day, he's a grandfather himself, and he said to me, 'I don't know what I'm going to do about my mom. She won't go to bed until three in the morning. She'll be up listening to the Redlegs. Games start at 11 p.m. and she never misses one.' And I said to him, 'Well, I think she's in her right mind. Leave her alone.' She and her husband used to go see the Redlegs, but the drive to Cincinnati got to be too much for them. Anyway, it's hard to get seats for the games now. Did you ever meet Waite Hoyt, Dick?"

Waite Hoyt for years was the radio voice of the Cincinnati Reds.

"Yes," I said. "A couple of times I sat in with him while he was broadcasting a game."

This impressed the poet no end.

"Oh," said Jesse Stuart, "he's the greatest. He'd sit up there and tell about everybody. And he would also talk Latin. What a tremendous announcer. I'm a real fan of his. He's a fine person, the finest. I remember how he used to talk about when he played baseball himself. He was something."

After a moment's silence, Jesse Stuart said:

"I'd just love to be seventeen again. I'd love to be out there, playing baseball, playing football, running track, all of it. I was in good health then. I just couldn't get enough to eat. I had ambition at that age. To win a game then was greater pleasure than to write a book now. I went after 'em and actually cried when we lost. Yep, when I was in high school I would cry when we lost a game."

"And the kids today?" I said gently. "Are they the same?"

He pondered this. A sadness came.

Then, a flicker of hope.

"Some of them are the same," he said. "I know because I had 'em and I taught 'em myself. Some of them are the same." But he had to be honest. This is the way poets are. "But the majority? No," he said.

"Things are changing?"

"A lot of things," he said. "Half the things they're doing these days are crazy. Like the bussing of kids to this school and that. Craziness. I think people ought to get along and I think they can. I don't think we ought to be fighting the blacks. I don't think the blacks ought to be fighting us. If we're true Christians, we can't be. We should know better."

"Where does Christianity fit?" I said.

"I don't fully understand it," the poet said, "but they're saying the blacks have a black god, the whites have a white god. That's what they like to believe, but I don't think we got either. From where Jesus Christ came from, I figure He must be brown. That's the way they are in the Palestinian area, you know. I know because I taught there. But let's get back to this other matter, Dick.

"We had a course in the Bible in high school and I figured something out once. We had a man who had a Baptist background but who had no Baptist church so he was going to the Presbyterian church. He fit in something wonderful down there in Greenup. He was a fine church man. Well, he gave us the course in the Bible. We learned all the books of the Bible, what each one was generally about, and it was one of the finest courses we ever had. In Ecclesiastes, I believe, Chapter twelve, we ran into something that stuck with me ever since. The Bible verse said:

The Kingdom of God is within you.

Don't you see, Dick. It was *within* me! So I got to thinking that anything could come *out* of me because I had that kingdom within me. It wasn't black or white anything. Do you see what I mean?

"I just recently found out that the Christian Science religion is based entirely on that view. I didn't know it before. I asked a real estate man up in Ashland—he's a Christian Scientist—what he would have done, though, if he would have had my heart attack. I wouldn't have gone without doctors. I had some excellent ones. The Christian Science religion is fine, but I just can't go for the fads and foibles. I told the man in Ashland that to do that would be contrary to nature."

He gazed at the house.

"We get 'em all here, Dick," he said. "We had some who were Jehovah's Witnesses. I've never seen anybody as hostile as those two. We sure had a time getting them out of the house, but they finally left. I said, 'You don't salute the flag. You don't fight for your country. What do you expect us to do to survive? *We're* making the world safe for *you!*' I told them that. Then, this lady spouted, 'Jehovah didn't do this and didn't do that' and I said, 'Lady, the Bible is filled with wars.' I said I read the Bible, too. I said, 'You don't take blood transfusions and you're against everything we stand for.' And I said, 'So I'm against you.' I said, 'Why do you come here when I've been in an established church for thirty years, a church I go to regular and help support? Why do you come out here to try to convert me?' They said, 'Why, you get literature from Texas.' I said, 'We don't get any literature from Texas.' See, Dick, that's one of the things they catch you on. I put 'em out of here, politely, but I put 'em out. What I'm saying is, there stands a warm house and we're friendly, but when somebody comes in and tries to convert me, old as I am, well . . ."

He threw up his hands in despair.

"But," I said, "you could sense the destruction of the house and its warmth?"

He nodded.

"Why my goodness," he said, "they could destroy it. We had a boy here at the time. He was Lee Pennington and he was working on a book and I thought there was going to be a regular fight. Listen, he despises people like that, coming in uninvited, destroying your privacy. Why would they come to us, of all people?" Jesse Stuart concluded, still bewildered.

"What is your religion?" I said.

"I'm a Methodist," he said. "Naomi Deane is a Methodist. My daughter is one, too. My mother was a Baptist. They quarrel all the time—Methodists and Baptists do. Also, my dad was a Republican and my mother was a Democrat. They quarreled all the time over politics. I once wrote a story about it. It was called 'Two Worlds' and published by the *Georgia Review.* It was a good story. You can't tell me two people that are opposites can't live together. My folks lived together forty-nine years and when my mother died, my dad grieved himself into his grave. Yet, they fussed and quarreled all their lives. They each had different ideas and held on to them strong. My mother, though, left the Baptist church, and the Methodist church has disappeared, so that leaves a Community church. . . ."

A diverse and independent man—that is Jesse Stuart. He is of diverse and independent parents. We adjourned to the house for lunch (Deane's homemade bread had turned out just right!), and afterwards we sat in the kitchen with Deane and got back on the subject of this diversity.

"Your mother and father apparently voted against one another," I said. "What about you two?"

Deane smiled. "I was a registered Democrat because of *my* parents' affiliation," she said. "But at our home, we never discussed politics. At least, my mother and father didn't in front

of us children. And when I was married, Jesse said, 'Now,
Naomi Deane, keep your registration, stay with it, because
we have friends on both sides, and it will never be an issue
with us.' And it never has become one," she added.

"And your daughter?" I said.

"When Jane could register and we were going to Egypt,"
Deane said, "we filled out those many forms, our religious
and political affiliations, you know. I thought Jane was going
to register as a Republican, like Jesse. Meanwhile, I had gone
down and changed mine to Republican because *I* wasn't
going to be the different one in the family. Jesse hadn't
known about it."

"I was sure surprised, yes sir!" said Jesse Stuart. "In her
whole family there had only been three Republicans before. I
wanted Naomi Deane to remain in her tradition. She was
born that way. And it's still a big Democratic county here.
The Democrats can win without effort here. The Republicans have to strain."

"So," I said, "you two never really voted against each
other, did you?"

Jesse Stuart shrugged. "No," he said. "I don't think so."
He looked at his wife. "What do you think?"

She smiled.

"Oh," she said, "we would discuss politics on election day
and I would ask how Jesse was going to do and he would say
he was going to vote for this and so. But he never asked me
to vote that way with him."

She looked at him with love.

"But I always voted his way," she said. "I just couldn't
vote against him. . . ."

Of his wife, the poet had written:

... I do thank God to have you for my own
To greet with April kiss and strong embrace ...

And, in W-Hollow, the afternoon deepened gradually into dusk.

THREE

"I WOULDN'T recommend that young people wait," Jesse Stuart said. "I've often said to my wife, I wish we had married sooner."

"Yes," said Deane. "Oh yes," she added with soft and Southern emphasis.

Then she smiled at Jesse Stuart.

"I wish we had married younger," the poet said, which summed up the way their love story was and is.

Twilight had come suddenly to W-Hollow. One minute it wasn't there, then there it was. Then just as quickly it turned into night—or so it seemed. Twilight still lingered on the high ground but in the hollow where they lived, tucked down inside, the night was black as the inside of a black cat. We three sat in the living room.

"What is your background?" I asked the poet's wife.

"My parents lived near Hopewell," she said. "My father was a farmer. We moved to Greenup when I was twelve or thirteen. He came here and got a job as shipping clerk at the Greenup Milling Company. I can still remember my mother and father discussing that move. He wanted to bring our family to Greenup so we would have better opportunities for school. And he worked there till he died. He didn't go to school much himself. My father had trachoma. He lost vision in one eye through a medication that a doctor in Cincinnati used. He had to stay in a dark room a long time. Then, he lost his vision completely."

"A fine man," Jesse Stuart said. "The finest man."

"Yes," said Deane. "Yes . . ."

When she spoke of the medication that had cost her father's vision, she spoke without reproach. Naomi Deane Norris Stuart speaks softly and with many smiles. For her to reproach anyone—even that distant and long-ago doctor—would seem to her unseemly. She is a hill-and-hollow noblewoman, a beauty who dwelt among untrodden ways. She has charm, the gift of silences, a sense of history, a sense of family, and through her the proud fabric of Kentucky runs strong. Some women grow old; others grow into greater beauty, and are therefore timeless. Two women I know have this quality: Deane and my own wife, Jean. Jean is still the refreshing imp of a charmer I first met years ago; she doesn't change. Deane is still the unvexed, untroubled and unbothered tall and slim Southern beauty whose smiles are like little curtseys.

"Where did you two meet?" I said.

"Right here in Greenup," Deane said. "In high school."

Jesse Stuart snorted. "Oh, I saw you long before you ever went to high school," he said. Love was in his voice. "I used to see you walking up that street. You used to go to Dilly's Store and we traded there, too. I used to just watch her, walking along the street, Dick. Tall, slender, beautiful girl. And later I was in high school with her. I was always conscious of her. Then later, after so many years, I claimed her and we married. We married kind of late. Most of our friends had already married, a few of them had even been divorced, but most of the marriages had stuck. And there we were, un-married."

"Well, I had a goal," Deane said. "Before I married, I wanted my degree. I taught ten years before I got it through summer work. I finished high school in 1928 and got my degree in 1938."

"I had come back from my Guggenheim Fellowship," Jesse Stuart said.

"And we were married in 1939," Deane said. "We corresponded all the time you were on the Guggenheim, Jesse."

"Our correspondence even made the papers," said the poet, excited about the recollection. "I saw that in a clipping, the clipping that said what little Greenup girl is going with a writer? Actually, it said what Greenup school teacher is going with a *beginning* writer," he added to keep the record straight.

Deane nodded, remembering, too. "He used to send me postcards," she said. "They'd be delivered to the dorm. You know the dormitory postal systems. The girls would all read the cards first. Very colorful postcards. From Scotland."

"That's where my dad's people came from," Jesse Stuart said.

"They were such pretty cards," Deane said.

They exchanged glances that were sweet and private.

The poet had once written of her:

Naomi Norris, we have gone together.
We walked together when the moon was full.
With hearts as light as a windswept fluffy feather—
Naomi, you were straight and beautiful.

You were as pretty as a maple tree
When its sharp leaves turn silver in the wind . . .

But Deane was saying to me, "I've taught thirteen or four-teen years in all, Dick. I finished teaching the year we were married. I didn't teach again until after Jesse's heart attack when he had gone to McKell High School as principal when the school was in trouble. It had fallen apart. I taught there because he hadn't been driving after his attack and we had about a fifty-mile round trip a day, so I taught a second grade that year. When we went to Egypt, I taught the second grade in a private American school for the children of the embassy personnel, but not all the time."

"It was a good school," said Jesse Stuart. "A top school."

"They had asked me to teach," Deane said. "I hadn't ap-plied. Jesse gave the commencement talk up there at that school for two cigars."

She grinned at me.

"How do you two work together?" I said.

"Oh," said the poet, "We work together. Tell him, Deane."

She seemed to shy away as if this would be intruding on the poet's accomplishments.

"He asks me to suggest what magazines might buy this or that piece of writing," she said. She sounded shy. "I'll read something he's written and he'll say, do you think it will go? I'm not a critic, but sometimes one guess is as good as an-other. I've been lucky. I've suggested markets that have bought his writing. . . ."

Her voice trailed off. She sought the background with si-lence.

"We have a division of labor around here," said Jesse Stuart. He spoke with enthusiasm and affection. "When we married we got up sort of an understanding. We wanted our marriage to be successful. She was thirty-one and I was thirty-two. She wanted to create a nice sight with the house, fixing it up and all. Let me tell you about those Norris women. They're all good housekeepers, aren't they, Deane?"

"Well, yes. My mother was interested in her home and family—and we grew up in that tradition," Deane said. She felt better. This was her domain. "My mother was attentive to my father's wants and needs and likes. I'm one of four sisters. I think we all have that same feeling toward our homes and our husbands."

"That's true," Jesse Stuart agreed, nodding his head.

"But," said Deane, "all I ever wanted was to stay here in the hollow and live on the farm."

"Did you want to leave here?" I asked the poet.

He made a helpless motion. "*I* wanted to leave," he said, "because I thought *she* wanted to leave. Yes, sir, I was going to be congenial and take her—not too far, of course— but where I thought she wanted to be. I didn't want to go to a town, but I would have gone with her."

"You see, Dick," Deane said, "then there were no conveniences here in the hollow. There was no road. On the first trips I made into the hollow, I walked in across the hill. So Jesse just didn't think I would like to live back here."

"My parents," said Jesse Stuart, "thought at first she was on the fragile side. They found out Deane was a person of endurance. Deane surprised all of them. But to bring her back here in this hollow where nothing was and her being a college graduate and school teacher . . ."

He peered at me as if to say, "You see the way things were, don't you?"

"We were married a year before we decided to come here to live," Deane said. "I was teaching when we were married. That was in October. Jesse was traveling, so we stayed at my mother's place. You were with Feakin's Lecture Bureau then, Jesse, and you had just finished *Trees of Heaven*. You had taken it to New York, they accepted it, and the bureau lined up a West Coast tour for you. Remember? He went by train, Dick. And I finished teaching that year. We still didn't know where we were going to make our home."

"Hadn't you two discussed it?" I said.

"We discussed it," Deane said, "but we didn't have any money."

"I was raising sheep then, too," Jesse Stuart offered.

Deane smiled at him. "Yes," she said, turning back to me, "Jesse had sheep on his father's farm. Jesse decided that we couldn't stay at his parents' home. And we had already been to my mother's. So we went and boarded at Fullerton for three months—and we just stayed there."

"We didn't have any place else to go," Jesse Stuart said.

"We came back on weekends to his home on the farm," Deane said. "But we had no car. Someone would bring us."

"I couldn't drive a car at the time," Jesse Stuart said. "I didn't like cars," he added.

"Then," said Deane, "we came out here one weekend and were talking with your dad. He said, 'Deane, you and Jesse want to get out to yourselves. You need to get out where you can wring your own dishrag.' I'll never forget that expression of his. So I said, 'You know, I think Jesse should stay here on the farm, on the land.' We got to talking about this

little house. It was used then as a barn. Hay and fodder were
in the first room you came in"—she pointed to the next
room—"and cattle had stood out back. It was after supper.
We got lanterns and flashlights and walked down here in the
dark. . . ."

She fell silent. Jesse Stuart, for a moment, did not fill the silence. They looked at each other, remembering. Their looks
were young. I sat, waiting, not about to break the spell. I sat,
surrounded by the ticking of the many clocks, and waited.
Then Jesse Stuart was saying:

"We had four cows down here. We had so much livestock
on the farm. All told, we had eighteen cows, fifty head of
cattle, and eighteen hogs which I think we killed that year.
We used to sell lard. And we used to make hams and shoulders. Also, we had three teams: one big span of horses and
two mule teams, a big team and a small one. We just didn't
have barn-room up there on the hill for all of those, so we
kept four cows down here in this old house. We've added on
a lot since, though."

In search of a final home, the Stuarts rolled up their collec-
tive sleeves and turned the log cabin barn back into the house
that it once had been. With a team of mules and a scraper,
the poet scraped away the animal droppings and straw.
"Scraped it right down," Jesse Stuart said, "and got her all
cleaned up." Then, they moved into the four rooms.

"I've always liked it here," said Deane. "So that night we
decided to move in. Jesse's parents were pleased that I liked
it. His parents were very encouraging, very helpful."

"Dick," said Jesse Stuart, "my mother just loved Deane!"

Deane modestly switched to another subject fast. "We just
came down here," she said, "and went to work."

Jesse Stuart would not let her hide her light under any bushel. "Dick," he said, as if they were both competing for attention to tell how wonderful the other was, "She came in here with her new ideas and everything—and here's the big thing of it. We came here with a plan: man and wife. I told Naomi Deane here, I said, *you* run the house. Whatever you have to have, I'll help you get it. I'll do my best. If I can't do it, it will just be impossible. You run the house, fix it up your way, and I'll be second when it comes to the house. Out on the farm, I'll be first. I know how to handle land. And you haven't done that, I told her. I'll run the farm, you run the house. I'll help you all I can with the house and you'll help me all you can with the farm." Jesse Stuart rubbed his head with satisfaction. "The plan worked out beautifully," he concluded.

"Oh, yes," said Deane.

"Were you surprised to find that you both wanted to stay here in the hollow?" I said.

"I was surprised to find that she wanted to," Jesse Stuart said. "I always wanted to. But I never wanted to leave Deane. I wanted to go out for her sake, if that was what she wanted, but I always wanted to come back. I always come back, don't I?" he added. There was a touch of melancholy in his voice.

"Yes," Deane said. She almost whispered it. "We both always want to come back."

A clock chimed. We waited for its chiming to end.

"We found out," said Jesse Stuart, "we had so many things in common: wildlife and plants and a nice home. I always *wanted* a nice home. Well, now you see it here. I think we've got it. And we made it ourselves. There's not another one just exactly like it. It is an original house."

"It just grew as our needs changed," Deane said. "And it grew as we were able to do more: added conveniences and added rooms."

Jesse Stuart laughed. "But, Dick, she does things that make me laugh. One of them is right behind you in the corner. I'd like to know how many times she's *changed* that corner to get it right. I'll see it changed and I'll say, 'Now what have you done!' And she'll say, 'Well, so-and-so wasn't the right thing for that place.' "

"Well," said Deane, "we've tried different pieces of furniture there, but after you brought those chests back from Korea, one of them just seemed to fit the space. It's a Korean sea chest, Dick. That's a betel box from Pakistan sitting on top of it. A betal-nut box."

"And those leather-bound books on it," Jesse Stuart said, "were bound in Egypt for about a dollar apiece. And then, there's that candle stand on it. And the ash tray from Korea. And that's a reproduction of a Grecian death mask...."

The corner, like the rest of their home, was dotted with souvenirs and memories and books, tastefully arranged everywhere. The odds and ends of their lives were on shelves and end tables and, as in the case of the corner, sitting on Korean sea chests. Jesse Stuart was right: this home was them. It could never be duplicated. But Deane is a master at arranging. *All* seemed right and *all* seemed comfortable and *all* seemed natural. What could have easily been the mustn't-touch mood of a museum had been turned by Deane into a home.

"What else did you try in your corner while you were experimenting with it?" I said.

"I had this little table there once," she said. She pointed to a little tea table that had been in her mother's home. "I did have a small chair there one time. In the beginning, Dick, we had difficulty filling the corners. But when we went to housekeeping we only had the four rooms here at first and that one little room upstairs. I had found and collected things before we were married, but the only thing you bought was the kitchen stove, Jesse. We had everything else we needed. It was a coal stove. A coal and wood stove."

"We burned wood in it," Jesse Stuart said. "I chopped the wood. Boy, you ought to have seen me down there chopping wood. There was once a picture in *Time* magazine of me chopping. I could sure use an axe. I've cut wood for the fireplace in this room, too."

"The fireplace in the other room and the kitchen stove," said Deane, "were the only heat we had our first year here. No lights, either. We used kerosene lamps and lanterns. We have a fuel oil burner now, but we still use the fireplaces all winter long. They're never closed."

"We'll have as much as twenty-four cords of wood up here," Jesse Stuart said, "and we'll burn that much, too."

"We're controlled by the location," Deane said. "We're surrounded by the hills—*and* the stream. How many times did we move that stream, Jesse, to give us room to build onto this side of the house?"

"Three doggone times."

"This room," Deane said, "and the bathroom and the new kitchen were added after the Second World War. Now that we've got electricity in the hollow we can have plumbing and running water. When we extended the roof of the back porch to add the kitchen, we found the cornerstone of the old log kitchen that was here when Jesse was a baby. You see, when Jesse lived here there were two log rooms. Where the dining room is now there was a breezeway, or dog trot, between."

Jesse Stuart nodded. "We used to stack our wood there," he said.

"But when I moved here," said Deane, "the old log kitchen had been torn away and the lean-to had been built across the back." She smiled at Jesse Stuart, then at me. "Jesse wanted just two things in our new home. He wanted wallpaper on the walls and white ruffled curtains. He likes the wind blowing through the ruffles."

"And," Jesse Stuart said, "I grew up in a house that didn't have wallpaper."

"And he didn't want the panels or the logs left exposed on the inside," Deane said. "He didn't want that rustic look. He wanted more."

"I'd like to know," said Jesse Stuart, "how many *Cincinnati Times-Stars* were pasted on those walls. That's the one paper Dad had. It was by the Tafts." He thought a moment and said, "We always had somebody living here with us. There were as many homeless people living here with us as there was family. Mom had them in. She sent them to school. My goodness, some of them stayed here and she raised them. No wonder we were in debt. Dad used to complain. He used to say he couldn't get out of debt at all, but my mother would just go out and bring in some more strays. I saw one girl the other day that they took in. I can remember she couldn't read and write when she came to our house here. My younger sister taught her letters from the bottom of her lunch bucket. Then they got her in school and she got a fair education."

"On the other side of the coin," I said, "did you have any
elders here with you?"

"Goodness, yes," said Jesse Stuart. "We had Uncle Jesse
with us twenty years. My grandfather was here twenty years,
too."

"And you had others," prompted Deane. "Wasn't there a
woman come by one time?"

"You're right. Annie Dysard. Had no place on earth to
light. She came in one night, carrying a baby in her arms. My
dad had been trying to find a girl to stay at our home. A
child was born. My brother Herbert, who's dead, was the
one. They didn't have any person here and Dad was trying
to cook and do the work and everything. He wasn't a good
cook, though. He just couldn't cook. And he had me and Sophia and two small children underfoot. Well, he took this
woman in. She started cooking. She had a boy about my age.
And did you know, she stayed with us and it just worked out
fine! But Dad thought of something. There was a man over
there that owned a farm, one of the Dysards. He and Dad
were good friends. And Dad knew Mr. Dysard needed somebody to help him. And by golly, my Dad got these two together. One of the best matches that ever hit the country.
We were inseparable, our family and theirs; we went back
and forth, and everything. I can see Mr. Dysard yet with that
horse he had. Gun Powder was the horse's name. And there
he'd sit up with that wooden leg stuck out like this. But I'll
never forget that dark rainy night when Annie and her boy
came to our door, homeless. The mother and baby had been
turned down by everybody. They had no place to stay. I
heard later she had some relatives in Raceland, but they

weren't there then. I don't know where she came from. Ashland maybe. Or Ironton. Or someplace. Dick, you never saw a house like ours. It was like a hotel!"

"How did you get any writing done back then?"

"In the smokehouse," said Jesse Stuart. "Then I built that bunkhouse up there in the yard. Later we put another room onto it. I had to get out of the house. You couldn't write here. You just couldn't. I did everything away."

"Could you write here when you and Deane moved back?"

That question seemed to make the poet sad.

"I could at first," he said. "Now it's getting so I can't write here any more."

"Why?"

"So many people. Dick, you've been here. You've seen 'em calling at all hours, stopping by at all hours. It's just a public place here."

I looked at Deane. "Is it rough," I said, "being the buffer?"

She seemed sad, too.

"It's hard," she said, "for me to say no to people who come to the door. It's hard for me to tell them he's not home when he is. I just can't do it. I just have to say that he's busy. The other afternoon he was resting and someone came—a cousin of his—and they hadn't been here before when we were home. Well, I just had to come and get him because it's hard to say no to people. But after his heart attack, we had to change. We changed our whole way of life. We three made an adjustment: Jesse, Jane, and me."

The poet fidgeted at the recollection.

"I was in that room there," he said, "cut off from people."

"Jane's room," Deane added.

"Why," said Jesse Stuart, awed, "I was just tickled pink to see anybody!"

"You like people," I said. "It must have been frustrating for you not to see them."

"Lord, yes!" said Jesse Stuart with emphasis.

"He was easily upset," Deane said. "You know, some conversations upset him and—"

"If you ever have a heart attack, Dick," Jesse Stuart said, warming to the subject, "you'll find out. Only I hope you never have one. It's very hard the first two years afterward to control your emotions. Doctors will tell you the same thing. And there are people who just naturally disturb you."

"Did many of the outsiders bother you those two years after your heart attack?" I said.

"No," said Deane. "Most of them were fine people."

"While I was in that room," said Jesse Stuart, as if indicating a prison, "I adjusted. I had gone quite a pace when that attack hit me. Naomi Deane was against me going that pace but in 1954 a dollar was a dollar. They were pretty good dollars back there in '54. I was doing two talks a day at five hundred dollars a talk. That's what I was doing. But I hardly got started on them. I was heading to California. Then I had the attack. It took two men to take over my lecture schedule," he added with pride.

"Can you control your pace now?" I said.

"I *try* to help him control it," Deane said. She sounded as if the task was hopeless. "It isn't easy to do, but we have learned to do it. I do suggest that Jesse not take on too many things or take things too close together. He's helped greatly in adjusting and setting the pace. All I could do is suggest and remind him he can't do as many things. And he'll say, 'Well, you're right.' "

I grinned at the poet.

"You," I said, "would be hard to slow down."

He beamed.

"Well, back then I was," he said. "For instance, one time I was flown by helicopter about Chicago to the different schools. Those were big talks. You ought to have seen the numbers of people I spoke to. I don't know why any of them turned out, but they sure as shooting did. I'd give three major talks a day. That's when they had the old airport on the South Side. It took me longer to get into the Loop at Chicago than it did to fly into there from here. I'd take a train to Charleston, then fly."

"Did you think you were indestructible?" I said.

Deane smiled at him. "Yes, he did," she said.

"But, boy," he said, "life was good and I was strong as an ox. That was my first time making a few dollars. I was going out there and getting a few and liking it."

"It makes sense," I said. "There is a momentum—"

"Oh, I don't lie about it," Jesse Stuart said. "I know some writers who say it's painful to write. And I always want to ask them why they write then. That's what I want to say. I don't believe them."

"If you don't have to write, I have been told," I said, "you shouldn't."

"Yeah," said Jesse Stuart, nodding his head in agreement. "You see, writing is an urge. It's an urge that's born in a human being. You've got to be born with it."

"So many people say to me," said Deane, "do I write, too. And I say no. I'm not compelled to. But Jesse *must*."

"Which of his writing is your favorite?" I asked her.

She stared at her husband thoughtfully.

"I don't know," she said at last. "I think I feel the way Jesse does about a lot of it. By the time we've finished with it—the proofreading and all—we're just tired of it, you know. You can't read it to enjoy it; you've worked on it so much. But of the poetry? I would say *Album of Destiny*. Prose? I would say *Year of My Rebirth*. I can't say why. Perhaps because I was more involved with it. I lived through it with him. And," she added, "I saw what writing it and keeping that daily journal did for him while he was in the hospital."

In the hospital, the bedridden poet had wanted his books with him and wanted his writing tools, too. He knew, then, his condition was critical. There had been a diversity of opinions from the doctors. But they said, bring his books to the hospital room. Put them on the table where he can see them. A long table was established in that room and on it they put all his writing things. He was still under oxygen, but whenever he opened his eyes, there was his writing world waiting.

"How many days *was* I under oxygen?" Jesse Stuart asked.

Deane thought a moment. "About thirty days," she said. Then she looked at me. "Soon he wanted to write letters. We would let him have just so much mail. He would dictate the letters to me. I couldn't take shorthand, though."

"I couldn't even raise my hand," Jesse Stuart recalled, impressed.

"So he started dictating some things that were very close and important to him," said Deane. "That's how *Year of My Rebirth* began. And then when he came home and could write a page a day, or two pages a day, he began doing that. It was therapy. It was the best therapy there was for him."

"January first was when I started," Jesse Stuart said. "I had the heart attack in October. Dr. Charles Vidt would allow me to write one page a day. He wanted me to take a rubber ball and squeeze it because I couldn't use my hand. But I said that was a waste of time. I said, let me write. He said, you can't write. I said I could. And he let me write one page a day with my right hand and one page a day with my left hand."

"You could write with both before?" I said.

"Yeah," he said. "If I wanted to. But I always preferred to write with my right hand. I bat left at baseball and do a lot of things left-handed. Pretty soon I was up to two pages a day with both hands, then three pages a day. Then I got so he let me flow. And I could just gauge how much better I was getting."

"But wasn't it frustrating to write a certain number of pages, then stop?" I said.

"Of course it was!" said Jesse Stuart. "Why, it was the worst thing that ever was. But I was tickled to death to get to do *that* much. There was a man come to me down at Murray. He was a big man and he was encouraging. He was a Seventh Day Adventist. He was one of the older ones there at the hospital. He said he was a surgeon during World War Two and that they put so much work on him he had a heart attack. He said he thought he would never use *his* hands again, either. He had heard about my hands. He was real encouraging. . . ."

We fell silent. We listened to the tick of the many clocks

and from outside the cry of the crickets, thousands of them in the hollow of night.

"I was in the hospital around fifty days," Jesse Stuart said at last. He stopped, Deane was looking at him.

"Forty-six days," she said and smiled.

"I was in the hospital forty-six days," said the edited Jesse Stuart. "Then they brought me home in the car. They didn't have an ambulance to haul me."

"They wanted you to sit up," said Deane. "They didn't want the vibration of a prone position."

"Anyway," said Jesse Stuart, "it was five days getting me here."

"They could only go so many miles a day," said Deane.

This was no quarrel. Each sang a love tune in counter-harmony with the other. It was a mature love tune and had with it great beauty.

"It was arranged," said Jesse Stuart, "so that I could hobble into the house here by putting my arms around her shoulders"—he looked at Deane with affection—"her shoulders and Nancy's, my sister-in-law. You know, Deane, I've always had such a warm feeling for her coming down like that and helping bring me home."

Deane smiled, said nothing.

A nagging thought struck the poet. "And Jane," he said. "What about our daughter? Was Jane with us?"

Deane nodded.

"Oh, yes," she said, her voice soft and Southern and sweet as ever. "Oh, yes, Jesse. Jane never left you. Jane stayed with you all the time. . . ."

And night—with tranquillity—consumed the hollow. Ten minutes later I was driving the hollow road back to the

country road. I could see nothing in the rear-view mirror.
The hollow was black. Where they lived was back there,
somewhere, around some dark bend. The hollow had for all
purposes disappeared.

A rabbit stared at the headlights in panic. I slowed to let it
flee.

That is the way love stories are.

FOUR

"I LOVE New York," Jesse Stuart said, "but I have seen her tumble."

Do meccas last?

Does each writer fall in—and out of—love with New York his own way?

Because now this poet from the land of stumps, rocks, wild roses, hidden hollows, burley beds, sudden twilights, and true furrows has no affection for New York. To him, it is a city with neither humor nor passion.

He peered across the room at me.

"Dick," he said, "do *you* go to New York much any more?"

When I said no, he nodded. My nod had made us lodge brothers, each suffering the death of the same dream.

It was morning in W-Hollow. In the kitchen Deane was making kitchen sounds. Jesse Stuart and I sat in the living room. Its hush was broken only by our words and the muted tickings of the clocks. He was subdued that morning. A tooth still hurt him enough to make him miserable.

Through the window I saw the morning breeze blow the cold, wet meadow grass. Fog made the meadow pale. Mist was everywhere, the corn bird had yet to fly and the day's brilliance was yet to be. To us, that moment, W-Hollow was real; New York was the unreality.

He rubbed his jaw and said:

"Do you know *why* we don't go to New York? Because they're incestuous there. They live in a circle, patting each other on the back, and the circle keeps getting smaller. This circle of theirs is all they got left. If you live west of the Hudson River, you're out of it. Golly, they at least used to have Boston with them. But they've cut off Boston and all New England, too."

This saddened him. Once, New York to him had been the land of literary giants.

"Another thing," he said, "have you ever had a book on a best-seller list?"

"No."

"Don't give it a thought," he said. "Neither have I. Best-seller lists are manufactured. Ralph Nader ought to investigate them."

"Georgia Glynn told me about how those lists are put together," I said. "She—"

"Did she tell you, too, Dick? Well, there you are!"

There you are, as someone once said, but where are you? Both of us believe in Georgia Glynn. Where best-seller lists were concerned, she knew whereof she spoke. Selling books had been her life's work. She ran the book department for many years in a Cincinnati department store. A shrewd book merchant, she had the ear of New York publishers. If she said a book would sell, the publisher would run with the book. If she said a book wouldn't sell, the publisher would back off from the book fast, the way a man does touching a red-hot stove. Few *real* best-sellers, she had told us, make most best-seller lists. When reporters call a store to see which book is selling best, she had said, chances are the book-store operator will look around to see which book isn't moving at all. Then, she will name that one in the hope that making a best-seller list will make it move off the shelves.

Can you see why most best-seller lists saddened Jesse Stuart, adding one more thing to the list of reasons his love affair with New York and its literary circle was over?

But it *had* been a dazzling love while it had lasted.

Picture this huge and boy-like mountain man going to New York when the love affair was young. He rode the C&O's *George Washington*, a most dramatic train. It left Cincinnati at suppertime, crossed the Ohio River to Kentucky, then followed the darkened twists and turns of the Ohio River Valley east. It thundered through Greenup at dark, shrieking wild hellos at unlighted crossings. Then it stopped for Ashland, Kentucky, where Jesse Stuart would get on, then whistle in its flagman, and head east into the black mountains of night. Back in mountain hollows, folks never heard its noise. Night had already claimed the convoluted land. All the hollow people heard were crickets and hoot owls and wind and—perhaps—the restless song of a nervous dove, sitting on a hickory snag.

But Jesse Stuart was in the lighted daycoach, heading to his love.

His passion for trains is equaled only by the passion Thomas Wolfe had for the midnight trolleys of Brooklyn. Jesse Stuart can't recollect how many times the *George Washington* carried him to Washington where, on another train, he continued his journey up the Eastern Seaboard—

hello, Baltimore! hello, Philadelphia!—to where Manhattan was.

Picture him at the breakfast hour, window-gazing from the *George Washington*'s magnificent diner as the diner lurches around mountain curves or smooths out on a straightaway. Dawn in mountainland. The diner—an eating palace on wheels. It is ornate and lavish and friendly. Its silverware jingles and jangles the railroad's tinkling tunes of knives and forks and many spoons. Dawn in mountainland. And there sits Jesse Stuart drinking tomato juice but unable to keep his gaze from the countryside the diner is hurtling by for his approval. Because he is of the land, he studies the land with the practiced eye of farmer-turned-muse. He watches for orchards and for fields. He is pleased when he sees fields that have been cleared of brush. He is saddened by the sight of fencerows in disrepair. He memorizes the crops and the wild flowers and trees that are lightning-struck. Dawn in mountainland. Then the land goes flat.

"I love trains," he told me. "Golly, I don't know how many states I've been through on them. Didn't they have wonderful names? The *Hummingbird?* And the *Dixie Flyer?* My breakfast on the *George Washington* was always the same: tomato juice, coffee, whole wheat toast, two eggs over light, bacon, jam, and biscuits. That was the best breakfast I ever ate. But that was when the train was running first-class. When I first started riding her, I used to sit up all night in the day coach. Later, when I could afford it, I would buy me a sleeper. I've been all through the South by train. I lost count of how many times I rode the trains in New England...."

Now he must fly. Luxury trains, like the little magazines that gave him sustenance, aren't any more.

Neither is the New York he used to know.

"When I first started going there," he said, "I would stay at the Prince George Hotel. It was near all the publishing houses. Cost me two-and-a-half dollars a night. Why, its dining room was so famous back then it seemed like everybody in New York City came of an evening to eat. Now I stay at the Woodstock where teachers stay. Everything is still close by."

The literary world of New York, for Jesse Stuart, is geographically small. It is possible, he says, to check into the Woodstock Hotel, conduct his literary chores, and never go more than six blocks from the hotel itself. Does the country poet go sightseeing? No. Once a body has visited the Staten Island ferry, the museums, the place where E. E. Cummings lived, and the crowds who create the Times Square midnight mood, what is left to see? Besides, in New York these days, Jesse Stuart is not a tourist. He is a writer with business to transact. To be a writer visiting New York is not to be a member of the American Legion in convention assembled. To visit New York as a working poet is, for Jesse Stuart, to be involved in an exhausting moment. Jesse Stuart the teacher is the gregarious Kentuckian. Jesse Stuart the poet is a recluse. Otherwise how would he find time to write?

The New York of Jesse Stuart's *other* years . . .

"Listen, I met Thomas Wolfe. I was at a few parties with him. I never saw a man in all my life who could drink the way he could. He was a big man. He was around six foot eight. Me, I'm six foot one, and there he'd be, standing over me, stuttering and sputtering and slobbering. Whenever he got a few dippers full, he would stand up there, his eyes looking wild, spitting all over you. It was like rain falling. 'By

God, Stuart,' he would say—and he'd start spitting, you know, and the rain would start coming down. Do you remember how he described the reptilian face? Well, you ought to have seen his face up close. And his eyes, black and sparkling. If there was ever a writing genius to hit the land, it was Thomas Wolfe. He was a natural."

"Was he as coherent in person," I said, "as he was on paper?"

"When he wasn't drinking by the dipperful," Jesse Stuart said.

"What other writers did you meet in New York?"

Jesse Stuart rubbed at his sore jaw.

"Well," he said, "let me tell you something. I have never sought out a writer. I'd be content to stand off and admire them, like I did Robert Frost. But I knew Frost. I knew Carl Sandburg. I knew Edgar Lee Masters very well. Masters is probably the most maligned writer of his age. I didn't know it but when I first met him he was suffering from malnutrition. I met him in 1939. He died in 1950. Deane and I used to take him out all the time, whenever we were in the same town. He was just a wonderful man. And there's Bill Saroyan."

"What was your first impression of him?"

"A handsome young man. That was when I first met him. Now he's got that big mustache. He was the sort of fellow who would jump up and take the conversation away from everybody. And to think, he only had a half a year of high school, but look at the stories of his in high school textbooks. You can hardly pick one up that he's not in. He's a natural writer. You've just got to hand it to him."

"And Robert Frost?"

"I loved him," said Jesse Stuart. "I don't think I've ever met a finer man. He was a great fellow with the young. He gave them good counsel. He was a fine poet, one of our better ones. . . ."

He leaned forward, bothered by the realities of being a poet in the world today.

"I wonder," he said, "how Robert Frost made it. Lectures, I guess. And Dartmouth paid him some kind of salary. But the point is, poets can't make it on their poetry. Carl Sandburg couldn't have. He got to lecturing, too, and went to Hollywood for a while. I talked to his son-in-law. His son-in-law told me Carl Sandburg wouldn't have made it if he hadn't gone to Hollywood. They paid him a pretty good salary out there."

"That's sad, you know," I said.

"Sure it is! Imagine a man like Sandburg and a man like Frost not being able to make it!"

The rural route delivery car stopped in front of the house. Jesse Stuart pretended it hadn't arrived, but he was impatient for Deane to go out to the mailbox, carrying her wicker basket, to return with the day's communications.

"One time the critics were really tearing me up," he said. "I was about to answer them, but Frost told me not to. So did H. L. Mencken. I knew him in New York back then. He was editing that big green-backed *American Mercury* and he said to me, 'Never answer them, Stuart. Let 'em have their say. Just let 'em go.'"

He watched as Deane returned to the house.

"Used to know Louis Bromfield, too," he said. "Listen, Ohio hasn't produced many writers in proportion to its population, but the writers it has produced have been fine ones.

Look at Sherwood Anderson. Look at the influence that man has had. There was James Thurber. And consider Bromfield with his Malabar Farm upstate. I know him well. I've been with him on many occasions. I've got all his books here. . . ."

Kentucky manners demanded he keep on talking, but the lure of the mail gave him the fidgets.

"Let's take a break," I said.

He was at the mail like a shot.

As he sorted through it, he kept up a running commentary to Deane all the while ("Deane, look who *this* is from. . . . Why, here's a letter from ——. I thought he was dead. . . . Here's somebody wanting me to speak"). I walked about the living room, preoccupied, pretending to be looking at the books on the shelves, but my mind was back in New York when Jesse Stuart was in love with all of it.

The literary giants have, for the most part, bitten the dust. All that remains are angry books or books filled with dark humor. The literary world is no longer gentle. But, on the other hand, was it ever gentle? I could see Mencken telling Jesse Stuart to ignore the critics. I could see Frost telling him the same. The critics back then had given Jesse Stuart a rough time. New York, therefore, is only gentle via recollection.

When the 703 sonnets called *Man with a Bull-tongue Plow* made the literary scene in 1934, they were both received and rejected. Mark Van Doren, writing in the *New York Herald-Tribune*, said of the book, "It ought to be interesting, even to those who think they cannot read poetry. They can read Jesse Stuart, if they please, as autobiography, and find themselves in the company of a modern Robert Burns." On the other hand, Malcolm Cowley, writing in *The New Re-*

public, said of Jesse Stuart himself, "He writes entirely too much for his own good or the reader's. At least half the time he is careless, trite or perfunctory; but always he is speaking in his own words about his own people, and he doesn't know how to lie." Horace Gregory, writing in the *New York Tribune*, said of Jesse Stuart, "His emotion is fluid, and his words are glib and careless; he tells you what he is about to say, and less often finds the time to say it." No, the New York of Jesse Stuart's love was not the gentle thing it is remembered to be.

Jesse Stuart settled in the chair across from me.

"Another thing about New York," he said. "There are places in Manhattan I'd never walk. It just isn't safe. In Rome and Athens I could walk anywhere. The same was true of Cairo. But not New York." He frowned at the thought of the danger. "It's not just New York, though. Some streets in Washington, D.C., frighten me. Louisville has streets I'd never walk. So do Cincinnati and Chicago. But New York *has* tumbled."

Each community has its own form of violence. Jesse Stuart admits this. The violence of certain sections of Manhattan, he suggests, could never equal the violence of the hills and hollows of eastern Kentucky. A mine disaster is a form of violence. So is the death of a tree. When Kentuckians assemble to celebrate, there is a joyful violence that comes if, upon occasion, some of the celebrants get sufficiently "lickered-up." Nor is the road that winds through the hollow any safer than, say, dark streets in a dark and angry city slum. Jesse and Deane Stuart are aware of any car that passes in the same way a tenement dweller is aware of an unfamiliar footstep in the hall. The Stuarts keep a shotgun handy in their closet.

The teen-ager carries a switchblade. Jesse Stuart understands this, but he *is* right: New York—and the world—have tumbled. The value of the straight furrow and the mended fence means little any more. It has vanished with the luxury trains, the trolleys, and the two-and-a-half-dollar room.

And the publishing world itself?

Jesse Stuart is melancholy about this: of all things that to him had value, the publishing world has tumbled the most.

"What I miss," he said, "is going to New York and seeing Ed Kuhn. He was a great guy, Dick. . . ."

Agreed. *Was* and *is*. But Ed Kuhn seems to have vanished into the confusion that is making hash of what had been a sound and thoughtful enterprise: the business of publishing books. Jesse Stuart feels this strongly. Ed Kuhn as Stuart's editor will visit the poet no more at the Woodstock Hotel. Ed Kuhn has given up the business of being an editor. He has chosen to stay outside of New York, within commuting distance of the city, and write. This saddens Jesse Stuart. Ed Kuhn was one of the best editors around, the poet insists. And I agree. He had been my editor, too.

Jesse Stuart and I talked an hour about the publishing business of now. Our conclusions: the publishing business is ailing, and what ails it, in our opinion, is this business of business—mergers and conglomerates and the rest. Great publishing houses were once rich with integrity—and little else. Now they are rich with money—and little else. When the accountant smiles, the poet does not. The truly good editors and truly good publishers have, for the most part, lost faith. When naked came the stranger, the good editors and good publishers left quietly. Publishing now belongs to the rack-jobbers, whereas it once belonged to beauty.

"You knew Ed Kuhn, didn't you?" Jesse Stuart asked.

I said yes.

Why do writers talk of departed editors as if the editors are dead?

"*He* is a professional," said Jesse Stuart. "When it came to books, you couldn't find a better editor than Ed Kuhn. Whit Burnett was the same when it came to magazines, but Whit didn't have the scope that Ed had. Ed was right up there in big business. He was in the middle of Big Time. He was really something."

"The editors today," I said, "are for the most part anonymous. Now the sales manager seems to run the store."

He nodded with vigor.

"You can say that again, Dick," he said. "They sure are anonymous. Look at ——— Publishing. Do you know any of the editors there any more?"

He had named a publishing house that had published both of us.

"The only one I know there is one I can't trust," I said. Once editors had been blood brothers. "He still owes me copies of my book and the book has been out six months. He keeps telling me they're in the mail."

"Ha!" said Jesse Stuart. "Never got 'em, did you?"

Lodge brothers again.

"Well," he said, "I never got mine from them, either. I had to go out and *buy* a copy of my own book to see how they had printed it! If McGraw-Hill had put out the book instead of them, the book would have made the best-seller lists—if the lists were honest. But the publisher didn't even bother to distribute the book in areas where my books sell well. Why, it was awful. One Knoxville store had one hundred orders for it they couldn't fill because the publisher never bothered shipping the books!"

We talked awhile—consoled one another would be more apt—about the merchandising and distribution side of the book publishing business. Most writers do. Merchandising and distribution concern writers almost as much as adverbs do.

"But we have to be concerned," Jesse Stuart said. "We have to be because the publishers don't seem to be. Golly, I don't think half of them know what business they're in." He rubbed his sore jaw carefully. "I'm inclined to think," he went on, "that the smaller publishing houses are better now for writers. The smaller publishing houses publish *and* distribute. And some of the smaller publishing houses have more time to give to the manuscript, the way Ed Kuhn used to do. . . .

Not all the good editors have vanished, we decided. Dan Wickenden, at Harcourt Brace Jovanovich, is one of the finest—and most sensitive—in the business. So is Sally Arteseros at Doubleday. So is Carol Cartaino at Prentice-Hall. They edit from the heart instead of from the cash register. But such exceptions each day, we agreed, get fewer. To find a good editor these days is to go among the corn by lantern light in search of a magic charm. Meanwhile the realities of the publishing business, of which we are a part, occupy much of our thoughts and days.

"New York!" snorted Jesse Stuart. "Oh, it may be fed by people from every state in the Union, but once they get jobs in the publishing business, something happens to them. They get together and form little cliques. Why, they're killing the publishing business, killing it dead."

"Do you work through an agent?"

"Not now, Dick, but I think I'm going out and get me one. That's one of the things Kuhn told me. Get an agent. He said the way publishing was going, a writer *needed* an agent. Why, would you believe I sent one publisher a manuscript and the publisher never even bothered to comment on it? I had been with that publisher for years, too. The book was all about snakes. Listen, it was dandy. I have a certain feeling about snakes, you know."

He grew reflective.

"Course, no one asked us to be writers, did they? It's something we *have* to do. When I teach creative writing at these seminars, I don't teach it. I let the students alone. If they're going to write, they'll write. Chances are, the ones who make it won't be the ones who edited the school paper. The writer will be someone you never expect, like the boy across the railroad tracks. *He* will be your writer. *He* will be your artist. New York, though, never sees this. But I'll tell you something. Ed Kuhn did. Ed Kuhn was special. Do you know what he told me once? And he's a practical man, too. He said, 'The best writers we get come through the school of hard knocks. They've never been specially trained at writing. They don't come out of writing workshops. At least, the natural-born writers don't. They're stronger and they're better writers, too.' He said Steinbeck was one of them. He said Hemingway was, too."

And Ed Kuhn had told me that Jesse Stuart himself was included in that list, but I said nothing. I sat, listening to the man who once called himself "a farmer singing at the plow." New York, as I suggested, seemed far away and unreal that morning. Outside, the sun had burned away the fog. The white windflowers waved. The sycamores seemed fresh and young again, warmed by the sunlight in the hollow. From the kitchen, where Deane was, came the scent of fresh bread baking. Outside the back window of the living room I saw the wind-dance of the ferns. And Jesse Stuart was saying:

"Ed Kuhn knows I've got four novels he would like to have. They're not written. I've got the ideas for them. But Ed Kuhn isn't an editor any more. Listen, if he was still an editor, there's no telling where I might have gone. He's the greatest editor I ever had. Why on earth they ever let a man like that get away I'll never understand. But he says it, too. The publishing business is sick."

Jesse Stuart looked sad.

"That group of people," he decided, "might just be too fast for Ed. . . ."

A word, here, about Ed Kuhn, please. He is a tall and thin creature with eyes that are huge and dark and warm. He and I have Cincinnati—and several books—in common. He is a Cincinnati native, too, now transplanted to New York. He loves Jesse Stuart. It is said that sometimes an editor will come along and make a writer look better than he is. This is the kind of editor Ed Kuhn is. With love—and a practiced eye—he takes a manuscript, separates the wheat from the chaff in it, sends it back to the writer along with a tender note, suggesting this or that revision. He has done this for me. He has done this for Jesse Stuart. We each have need of such an editor because we each, as writers, gush out words that are sometimes too much and too many. We are mountain creeks, gushing with the torrents of the mountain rain; his editing and suggestions reduce us again to gentle streams that have meaning and value, if any should exist in what we write.

Ed Kuhn has, as I have, sat in this room with the tickings of the many clocks. As an editor, he has quarreled many times with Jesse Stuart. But the quarrels have all been gentle. Ed Kuhn has, as I have, seen the thousands and thousands of pages of unpublished manuscripts that Jesse Stuart, that sly farmer-poet, has stored away against the winter. Ed Kuhn has rummaged through this verbal torrent with affection and a professional eye. "Let's try this one," he would say to the poet. Or, on the other hand, he might say, "Let's sit on this one a little longer. All right?" This was his way of saying no. A good editor does not bruise a poet, for poets, in spite of their years of mending fences, bruise easier than apples do. The sensibilities of a good editor are fine-tuned to the passions of the poet whom he must edit. Ed Kuhn has sensibilities to spare. He could respond to the cry of any true writer —and respond with charm, intelligence, and soul.

Yet, I wondered with a sadness that was acute, if Jesse Stuart had ever heard his editor say no. Jesse Stuart brims too much with life. The thunder and the rain in him, via words, must gush out. He must write of hills lined with pine and gum and black-oak trees. He must write of scrubby pines, ghosts of timber roads, buzzards, honeybees, clapboard shacks, pitchforks, and potatoes in the hole. Just as the winds of winter clear the trees of branches that are dead, so an editor clears the poet's torrent of verbs and adjectives and moods and pointlessness. Ed Kuhn, that thoughtful pruner, was Jesse Stuart's winter wind. Now Jesse Stuart sits in his well-tended hollow, brimming with a thousand poems yet to be written, and has no editor to say, with a gentle voice, "Let's sit on this one a little longer. All right?"

"Did you," I wanted to say to Jesse Stuart, "ever hear Ed Kuhn say no?"

But that was a question I never asked.

"I went to New York on my first trip in 1935," Jesse Stuart was saying, "a year after *Man with a Bull-tongue Plow* was published. I couldn't stand the big city. I moved out and went up to New England. I went to Concord, a city of writers I'd studied. I went into Maine so I could say I'd been in Maine. That first trip was one of the most fabulous journeys I ever took in my life. Why, I looked up where Longfellow was born. I went to the coast and sat around, talking to teachers. I even tried to get a job teaching up there."

He had cheered himself again.

"Portland, Maine," he exclaimed. "Everybody tried to be a writer up there."

Deane entered the room quietly.

"I looked at Walden Pond once," Jesse Stuart was saying. "It's got scum all around it. Or did have. They got it cleaned up a little, but it was awful. Trash thrown everywhere. You know, Dick, Massachusetts isn't the best state in the Union. It's . . ."

"Now, Jesse . . ."

Deane spoke softly. The perfect editor.

I could picture them both in New York back then when New York was sweet and magic. I could picture them strolling Broadway hand in hand. She would be the tall and slim young Southern lovely, every inch a lady; and he—well, he would be talking a country blue streak as this or that Broadway wonder—the cop on the horse, the billboard that puffed smoke rings—presented itself for his pleasure. I could picture them waiting in hotel lobbies and restaurant lines and in reception rooms of publishing houses. Jesse Stuart, wherever they were, would be engaged in conversation with either his lovely Deane or the thousand New York characters met by chance contact: elevator operators, taxi drivers, busboys, receptionists, and, perhaps, literary giants. Jesse Stuart could no more pretend to be the New York sophisticate than he could let a pitchfork rust. And always beside him, Deane, his editor and his love, talking at him with words—when she could get them in edgewise—or talking at him with her eyes.

For the secret of Jesse Stuart is this: whenever he went to New York, he took W-Hollow with him. As he changed trains in Washington's great terminal—bidding the *George Washington* goodbye, climbing aboard the New York express—he wore forever the protective cloak of the hills and hollows of home. He wrapped around himself the solemn mood of dying soapstone oaks and he took with him the memory of ferns and vines and burley beds up on the hill. Although the noise of grunting shoats and rain on clapboard shacks would be replaced by the bedlam of Broadway traffic and the traffic cop's whistled tweet, the secret of Jesse Stuart in New York is that he never truly left home. What he was, he still is, and what he still is—poet and farmer and overgrown boy—makes him forget that New York in those early days was not as sweet as remembered.

And New York publishing? Has it tumbled? Yes and no. And New York itself? Has it tumbled? Well, yes. And thus the poet in Jesse Stuart is sad.

> *... The call to earth is pounding in my brain,*
> *I want to walk with my bare feet on earth,*
> *I want to go back to the earth again ...*

FIVE

NOW here's a country cemetery," said Jesse Stuart, "that has probably more characters in print than any I know."

"In some way," I said, "they're all still living—out there somewhere, on library shelves."

"You're right," he said. "I guess they are still living. . . ."

We stood that morning at the iron-fence entrance to Plum Grove Cemetery. The hill we were on was not as high as the others that surrounded us. The church—the "new" church—was at our backs. And the morning fog still lingered in the valleys strewn down there before us. We could see toy roads and an occasional toy house. But where we were, silence reigned. We were surrounded by the past, bushes that pawpaws grew on, a few trees—the cemetery hill has been pretty much cleared—and the moist, cold breeze of morning.

Plum Grove Cemetery, unless your kin sleeps there, is the duplicate of thousands of country resting places that have country churches adjacent. The cemetery is no bigger than a lot in the suburbs. It contains a variety of headstones. Some are old and almost illegible. Some are new and fresh. Where the school had been, part of the cemetery now is. Where

Jesse Stuart would rest, when God called, was the exact spot where, as a boy, he sat in the back row of the one-room school and gazed out the window at the rain and snow and seasons of yesterday. When that final moment comes, the muse will have completed the circle.

The Plum Grove Church itself has changed. It had once been crude and beautiful plank and weatherboard. Now it has been modernized. But inside? "They took the lumber out of the old church, which stood right where the new one does," Jesse Stuart said, "and put it back inside. You ought to see the inside of it, Dick. For a little country church, it's beautiful. . . ."

The church was locked tight, though, and we could not enter. Besides we had many friends to visit, all of them sleeping. Here, on this small hilltop, Jesse Stuart as a lad chased ground squirrels and over there the baseball field had been. Here, now vanished, enormous oaks stood—eight feet through, some of them—and as a boy he had sat on their huge roots to see teams pull wagonloads of coal up the township road that isn't there any more except in memory. As many as sixty children at a time had come to that one-room school where Everett Hilton taught everybody, from the first grade through grade eight. Now all have said their goodbyes and have scattered in the wind. And here now, Jesse Stuart, strolling among the headstones of his friends.

"There's some still living hereabouts who say they don't want to be buried here where old Jess Stuart will be buried. They say they figure they've been written about. The funny thing is, they *have* been written about, too. But I never wrote mean about anybody. I never wrote vindictive.

"An artist, Woodi Ishmael, came up here with me once.

That was when the big trees were still standing. He laid down on his back on the grass and he said of all the places he had been on earth, this sure was a dreamy place here on the hill. He's right, too, isn't he?"

Jesse Stuart paused before one stone.

"Here's my mother's grave and here's my father's. Now here's where my brothers are buried. Herbert Lee Stuart and Martin Vernon Stuart. Herbert was born in the house where my sister Sophia lives now. That's where he was born. The only place the little boy lived was there. He was a handsome child. I wish I was artist enough so I could draw him. I would draw his picture. He had black curly hair, real wavy, and brown eyes. A most handsome child, Dick. I have such good memories of him. I was three years older than he was. He died when he was five. Martin was hardly here at all. He died at two months. They both died of the same thing. Some kind of fever . . ."

He moved, with restlessness, to another stone: the stone that marked his mother's grave.

"I've done her in *Bull-tongue Plow*," he said.

> *And you, my mother, who will stack by you?*
> *In beauty—yes—others are beautiful*
> *And you are not in flesh and fancy guise.*
> *But you have lived a life so rich and full,*
> *Few wordly beauties stack beside you. . . .*

He didn't look at me. He looked at the stone that marked her grave. He said, in a low voice, but quickly, as if to break the spell, "And that's the way they go, Dick. There are poems for my dad, too. He—" Jesse Stuart stopped, stepped

quickly over to another stone, and as if to erase the memory
of the goodbyes he had once said on this hill, pointed to the
stone and said:

"Now *there* was a woman, Dick. This one here drank kerosene! I wrote about her, too, but didn't use her name. She
chewed tobacco, too. I don't know how she lived, drinking
kerosene, but she sure did. She was an odd one around these
parts. This was back in the days before electricity. She would
go to the store and get a can of coal oil for the lights—and
turn up the can and swig it right out of the spout!"

His tone was lighter. The spell that had troubled him before had been talked away.

We paused before another set of stones.

"Here's my mother's father, right here," he said. "He's
been in my stories. Died in 1943. If he had lived a couple
more months he would have been ninety-three years old. He
was the most powerful man, physically powerful, I ever
knew. He weighed two hundred and forty pounds. I helped
him hew trees to make our first house. It nearly killed me
working with him. Powerful! He could lift the end of a saw
log. And, Dick, he was considered an old man even then. I'm
strong. I used to be able to lift four hundred pounds up from
the ground, but I could never compete with him. Why, one
time he lifted up a big rock, set her on the wagon, and the
rock was so heavy it went right through the wagon floor.
Orville Griffith down in Greenup says he used to watch my
grandfather load telephone poles by himself. Strongest man I
had ever seen. And he never had false teeth. He chewed tobacco with his teeth at eighty-eight years old. He quit work
at eighty-eight because he had to, his legs came down on him.
The last five years of his life he wept, wept because he

couldn't work. Then, one night, he died peaceful. In his sleep."

His other grandfather?

"I don't know where he lies," Jesse Stuart said. "My grandfather Stuart was a Union soldier and a good one. My grandfather buried here was a Confederate soldier but he wasn't too good at it. He didn't want to kill anybody. There's no record of any homicides among the kin on my mother's side of the family. They're like Quakers. Oh, one hit a man with a car, by accident, killing him. I think it was one of my cousins—and my uncle made him take the car out of his sight. They just don't kill. There's a lot of that in me, too. But my father's side of the family—the Stuart side—is different. A Stuart is a doer. They were all soldiers. They *all* fought for this country. I don't believe there was ever a family from the North or South that ever fought for America like the Stuarts. They've been getting killed in wars since the Indian Wars of 1740, the year they came to this country. But I don't know where my father's father is buried. Somewhere along the Big Sandy River where he was killed. Dad and I went up there once hunting for his grave but we never found it anywhere. . . ."

He looked down at the valley farm below us. The farm was just presenting itself, having freed itself of hollow fog, as if brushing the night away.

"See that tobacco down there?" Jesse Stuart said, pointing to a toy field. "That is a land-grant farm the people got for fighting for the country. The same family still owns that land, only here, right here"—he pointed to a grave—" was the last male amongst them. There are no male descendants left. When a couple of the ladies pass on—and they're real old now—the land will go to somebody else, and that will be the end of it, won't it?"

The tombstone said the man, named Dysard, was born in 1828, but Jesse Stuart said the family went back way before that. There were many Dysards sleeping on the hill that looked down on where their farm was. Jesse Stuart said he himself was a tiny boy when one of the Dysard men died, a man in his nineties. They hailed from Greenburg County, Virginia. Dysard women were sleeping beside their husbands. Dysard babies, plucked young from earth, slept beside their parents. Soon they would *all* sleep there, the final gathering of the clan.

"See how well this cemetery is kept?" Jesse Stuart said with country pride. "Have you ever seen anything better than this? For a country cemetery, I mean. The people around here are industrious. They take care of things." He stopped before another stone, looked at it thoughtfully, and then moved off elsewhere among the stones. I wandered after him. The poet stopped, looked about, puzzled.

"What is making that noise down yonder?" he said.

A buzzing sound had interrupted the hilltop silence where only wind and the cricket's call had been before. We stared down into the toy valley so far below us.

"It's a tractor, isn't it?" I said.

"I see it now," he said. "It's pulling a load of tobacco."

He stared at it, then looked away, as if the tractor was of today and had broken the spell. As we passed this stone and that one, he recited the tragedies of the hill-and-hollow people. This one here got hit by a train. That one drowned in a creek. This one died from too much drink. The fever made that one die. From each grave ghost whispers seemed to say:

"Yes. That's the way life did us."

We paused before one stone.

"That's an unusual name," I said.

"Sini Young," said Jesse Stuart. "Died in 1934. My dad used to haul for her. She lived right down there on that other farm yonder. I didn't know William Young. He died before I was born. And look, she outlived him by thirty years. A rugged old lady. Ran the farm by herself. That man over there," he said, pointing to another stone, "used to play with me but he went to Illinois, where he died, shucking corn. This other one here—he was a Civil War veteran. His stone sure needs fixing, doesn't it? Well, we'll get it fixed if I have to do it myself. That one over there was another friend of mine. Wild as a buck."

"What did he do?"

"Whatever he could, but mostly he drank," said Jesse Stuart. "I think that maybe what made him go to drink was tuberculosis. Now this one here was big and husky. But he died of tuberculosis, too. This other one, though, got drowned putting in a high-level dam. Got his boots full of water and drowned. I remember when this one was buried. I came out here and sort of directed. His folks didn't come any farther from yonder where they had buried their other sons. They just couldn't. They had lost all their children but one. They had had ten. But nine died. The mother, though, lived to be eighty-six years old. A doctor told me once she was a germ carrier. She never had active tuberculosis herself but she carried the germ. That's what the doctor said anyway. He said there were people like that. And half her children died of it."

Sini wasn't the only unusual name. The stones announced

the resting places of ladies with first names of America, Kansas, Kentucky, and Missouri. Said Jesse Stuart, "There's a lot of women here that have been named for states."

Do you remember the last scene in Thornton Wilder's play *Our Town?* The dead sit in rows on kitchen chairs, commenting on and regarding the living who visit their graves. Jesse Stuart, through his words and moods, made the Plum Grove dead rise from their graves, too. As we moved among the stones I no longer moved among bodies turned to dust but among people—all sorts—sitting on kitchen chairs, looking at us with sadness and with wonder. For each, the personal tragedy of departure had dimmed and they seemed surprised that Jesse Stuart attached meaning to that triviality called death.

"Here was another family," Jesse Stuart was saying. "We used to go visit them. That boy over there"—the one staring amiably at us from the kitchen chair—"was driving home from work, his car turned over, he got into a bit of water, and he drowned. The other one"—sitting on his kitchen chair but ignoring us—"fell on the street in Greenup and hit his head on a curb when he was going to school there. He became a mental and he died awful young. The other boy died working. One got killed in the war. All the boys in that family died and there wasn't anybody left."

Jesse Stuart stopped before one grave. He looked at it attentively. The farmer, wizened, sitting on the kitchen chair atop the grave, had no eyes for the poet. He gazed, instead, down into the valley, keeping eternal watch on his farm.

"Henry Wheeler," Jesse Stuart said. "He died when he was seventy-three years old. He was the workingest and the

savingest man. He knew how to till the land. That's his farm
down there. It used to look like a park. Beautiful buildings,
all kinds of barns. He was a man! Oh, he didn't believe anything in religion. I got a bunch of poems about him, but I
don't think he would have liked 'em."

Mr. Wheeler gazed at his farm, chewing his eternal wad,
ignoring the song Jesse Stuart sang of him.

> *Now he belongs to Plum Grove's rotting dead*
> *And he lies silently upon this hill.*
> *And I remember many words he said*
> *Before his brain was dust and tongue was still.*
> *"See here, my friend, I tend my business here.*
> *I have my land. I raise my grub to eat;*
> *And I been here nigh onto seventy year.*
> *I raised nine children, put them on their feet.*
> *I never go to church—I do not pray.*
> *See here, my friend, my church is in the woods.*
> *On Sundays I get out and spend the day*
> *In the green temples—God's cool solitudes.*
> *See here, my friend, I'm just Anice Bealer;*
> *A damn good farmer and a cattle dealer . . ."*

"He died," the poet said with finality. "He was both fine and
coarse. He talked real fine to you and then he would come
around and rise up in a husky voice. He was an oddling."

"What do you suppose he would think of his farm down
there now?" I said.

"Why," said Jesse Stuart without hesitation, "if Henry
Wheeler was back here the first thing he would do would be

to clean up that farm. He'd never let it go the way it has gone. Those fencerows would be all cut out. The place would be like a park again."

We continued to stroll among the stones and the dead who watched us almost absently.

We passed the graves of two brothers who had died the same year. Their father had been a coal-mining man. The boys were husky lads. They watched us but did not seem to care.

"A good family," said Jesse Stuart. "Those were strong people. They were not school people, though. They were all coal miners. We passed their farm coming over here. Handsome people! And the girls among them were the prettiest around here. They were like Greek statues. Right here is where I met most of them, right here on this very hilltop."

At another grave, Jesse Stuart said, "That's Hiram Kiser. We used to call him Dink. And, look, there's Henry Calahan. He was a little short fellow. Never married. They were Methodists. With a name like that, he was as Irish as he could be. He dug more graves out here in his lifetime for people —and dug 'em all free. Only one day he was digging out here, got hot, drank too much water, and died. He was the workingest little man you ever saw."

At another grave, Jesse Stuart said, "This one here used to walk clear into Greenup to get a magazine or a newspaper to read. Right there he lies. He was an infidel of the community. I've got him in *Bull-tongue Plow* somewhere."

At another grave, Jesse Stuart said, "Now these people here were most wonderful. The old man was kind of crazy but I liked him. When he'd get liquor, he'd be wild. But when he was out of liquor, he was nice as pie. This here is where his son lies. He was a beautiful boy. Blond. Blue eyes. Only he died when he was young of tuberculosis."

At another grave, Jesse Stuart said, "I knew this man and I liked him. Now, I'll declare, though, he was a colorful character. He could put away the whisky. And he could doctor the cattle. He loved doctoring the cattle. He had every kind of veterinary book in the country and he knew them cover to cover. If he had been educated, he would have been a topnotch veterinarian. Oh, he was a doer, all right. I knew him. I knew his family. They're all buried here. He married twice. There's his first one. There's his second one. . . ."

At one grave, the poet and I got involved in "new math" and lost. We were trying to figure out how long John Griffith had lived. Born in 1873, he had died in 1952. Here is the actual conversation from the tape.

JESSE STUART: Let's see, Dick. 73 would be 29. 29 and 52 would make it 81, wouldn't it? 2 from 3 is 1, and 5 from —no, wait a minute. 2 from 3, and 5 from 7, is 2. (Pause) What am I doing? It should be the other way around.

PERRY: Let's see. Add 28 to 52 and we've got it. 28? No, add 27.

JESSE STUART: 27? Well, 27 and 50 . . .

PERRY: That's 59. No, it's 79!

JESSE STUART: Yeah. You put the top down below to subtract. 3 from 12 would be 9, and 7 from 14 would be 7. 79 *is* right!"

John Griffith, sitting on his kitchen chair atop his grave, seemed to frown a seventy-nine-year-old frown at both of us!

"There are certainly a lot of interworkings of families in this graveyard, aren't there?" I said.

Jesse Stuart agreed. "They're all kin and tied up nearly," he said. "What I mean is, there's certain groups tied up here. There's whole families here. And isn't it strange? I knew them all! And look at the stories and poems I've gotten from these people. And right here they all are!"

They didn't seem impressed. They seemed preoccupied with inner thoughts. We were, to them, no more important than the corn bird that darted by.

"But you wrote nothing about them to hurt them," I said.

"I can truthfully say that, Dick," Jesse Stuart said. "I have not hurt a one of these people. Not a one. I liked 'em. I liked 'em all! I wrote about my uncle and there he is. I wrote about him letting the weeds take the corn while he sat and read *The Decline and Fall of the Roman Empire*. He'd get into a book and let the crops go. He read all the time. He got intrigued with *Tarzan of the Apes*. He read all these different religious sects and studied them thoroughly. And now yonder he is, right there."

His uncle did not look up from his book.

We passed his stone and wandered elsewhere.

Jesse Stuart said, "There's actually four books up here in this cemetery, besides scattered short stories and poems. Who'd ever think that about a little country cemetery? This is a little place, too, isn't it? You take that boy there. He was a nice boy. His father was a coal miner and my dad dug coal with him many times. That boy got hold of some dynamite powder, happened to strike a match, and burned himself up. He had been a handsome kid. He was only eleven. . . ."

The sweetness of the cemetery was laced with the violence

that brought its people together. Yet, those assembled on
their kitchen chairs, some watching us, others not, seemed beyond the violence and the sweetness, beyond all of it.

"There," said Jesse Stuart. "Look there . . ."

Was it eight or was it ten small babies, hardly born, sitting
in a row?

"They kept telling the mother of these babies," said Jesse
Stuart, "that she couldn't have children. But she went on and
tried anyhow. The whole row of them yonder all died in in-
fancy. But she wouldn't take no for an answer. She kept
trying and she got one. She raised the ninth one, I believe.
These were real country people, poor; they dug and grubbed
the poorest fields in the county. But this baby they got, this
daughter, turned out so beautiful. She grew up, got married,
and left."

But Jesse Stuart had been avoiding one section. He could
avoid it no longer. There were no other sections left to visit.
His voice was low as he said, "You know, this will be sacred
ground for me. Here's my lot and there's Deane's. Right
here . . ."

Silence.

I said, "What are your thoughts as you—"

He interrupted. It was the only time, in the many hours of
conversation, he had ever intentionally interrupted me. But
the mood was one beyond the call of Kentucky manners,
wasn't it?

"I just forget about it," he said fast. "I forget about it like I
do the legend thing. But anyway, here's where it will be,
right here. And here's where the school used to be. There
was the recitation seat where we used to recite, yonder,
where my mother and father are buried. Is there any signifi-

cance to that, them being buried right there? And here's where I used to sit with old Corby, the back of the school, right where I will be buried. His folks were from the coal fields back in the buzzard-roost country. Even then this one hill was cleared but the other wasn't. . . ."

He stopped talking for a moment. Again he had successfully talked himself out of a mood. He was himself once more.

We closed the little iron gate—it squeaked—and crossed to the church and to the new graves that were planted behind it. Jesse Stuart gazed about at these graves— and the friends who sat on kitchen chairs above them. At one, the poet paused.

"This one here," he said, "was my closest friend. Lived in West Virginia. Left here, but grew up in these hills. Oh, my goodness, he was a character. But there he lies. Him and another boy came out here once and lived together. They were some boys. From the time he was in grade school he was never without a pistol. One night, when we were all in church here, somebody threw a rock through the window, just missing my mother. We were having some kind of church service there. And this boy, he jumped up and ran out and he pulled out his pistol to shoot the rock-throwers, only the minister ran out, too, and the bunch that had thrown the rocks was running down the hill, and the minister knocked his arm up in the air, saying, 'You can't do the Lord's house this way!' If the minister hadn't done that, some of the rock-throwers would have been killed. He was some boy."

"When did *you* quit shooting?" I asked.

"Way back there," Jesse Stuart said. "I was an excellent shot, too, though not as good as he was. My brother James was better than I was, too. He could throw a marble up and crack it with a rifle. There's a secret to it. He'd wait until the marble got up there and hung. He'd follow it and just as quick as it started to come down, he would squeeze the trigger and break it all to pieces. Boy, what a shot. He was a gunnery officer in World War Two. He went in on those little motorboats to knock the pillboxes out. . . ."

Our visit to Plum Grove cemetery was over.

As we walked back to the car, Jesse Stuart, strangely exhausted and strangely at peace, said, "Well, Dick, that's Plum Grove. What do you think of it?"

"Beautiful," I said, "in a personal and private sort of way."

"Do you know what they call cemeteries in Egypt?" he said. "They call them 'cities of the living dead.' I think that's nice, don't you?"

I agreed.

As we got in the car I looked back at the graves and the Kentucky people sitting on their kitchen chairs. The sun was bright but they did not seem interested. I thought I could hear wind-murmurs of their conversations—but this is poetic foolishness. They were not there at all. Jesse Stuart had written it better when he once wrote:

> "Oh, take a rest," I know the wind has said.
> "Lie still," the ferns have said, "there is a reason."
> Muscles are lifeless in a body dead—
> A body dead and corn sprung from its bosom.
> "Lie there," a gray stone said, "the best is over."
> "I'll pin you down," oak limbs have said to me.
> "I'll make a quilt for you," said the green clover
> "If I don't spindle under this shade tree."

'I love dirt lips," the green briar roots did say,
"I love the heart and ribs and slimy eyes."
"Now, I shall hold you down," said the warm clay.
"I'll hold you down so you can never rise."
Now if there is a Resurrection Day
Will you be one that's taken by surprise?

The Plum Grove dead are dead. At least, their bodies are
buried on that pennywhistle hill where once a one-room
schoolhouse stood. But as Jesse Stuart and I drove down the
rutted road, leaving the cemetery behind us, passing the un-
kempt fencerows that Mr. Wheeler watched with eternal
sadness, I sensed the dead of Plum Grove would never be
dead as long as Jesse Stuart's books were in classrooms and on
library shelves. Nor were the long-ago coon dogs dead. Nor
were the long-ago cloudbursts and the snows. I listened to
Jesse Suart continue his soliloquy as he drove by Wheeler's
place.

"Henry Wheeler wouldn't allow brush along here," Jesse
Stuart was saying. "That would all be clean. And neither did
the Coopers allow brush when they owned the farm. But isn't
this just beautiful along here? The fencerow should be out of
there, though. All of that should be torn out. I'd bulldoze
around here, it's quicker, and sow it with grass. . . ."

Farther down the hollow road, Jesse Stuart said, "Now this
used to be a cornfield and the family that used to live in that
house—why, I've written stories about them, too. This
road isn't too good in winter. Sometimes in winter it would
still be impassable. You swam your car through mud to make
it through to the cemetery. But you got there. You got there
eventually. . . ."

Yes, Jesse Stuart, yes.

And now I shall speak back to my own hills
And say farewell to them—these hills I love;
Farewell to hills of phlox and daffodils;
To rugged hills and flying clouds above;
To hills broad-shouldered and the deep ravines;
And sky-blue mountain water leaping rocks.
Farewell to rock-cliff ribs and scrawny pines;
Farewell to stubble fields and fodder shocks—
These are my own Kentucky streams and hills.
Kentucky's womb gave blood and flesh of mine
Where men still unafraid will shoot to kill;
Where men still clear the dirt of briar and bush;
Where strong men clear earth and use bull-tongue plows;
And make their bread by the sweat of their brows . . .

The Plum Grove dead, sitting on their imaginary kitchen chairs, did not wave goodbye to the Plum Grove poet. Instead they settled back on their chairs again, knowing he would return.

SIX

WE turned off the county road into the winding road that fidgets its way through W-Hollow. The mood of the cemetery visit still lingered, but we talked about a bunch of other things because that is the way men are.

"Are people leaving these valleys?" I said.

Jesse Stuart nodded.

"They have to," he said. "They get such education, they're bright people now. So they have to go away to put it to use. But in fifty years I figure this valley will be filled with homes. People *want* to come here. Here is where the residential building sites will be. Boyd County, east of us, is industry. Greenup County here is getting to be industry, too. Back here is where they'll want to come and live. Yep, this valley will be filled with homes in fifty years."

Sly old poet—or lonely man contemplating the end of a dream? Had he, as some imagined, accumulated the 1000 acres of W-Hollow against the day people would buy bits and pieces of it for plots upon which to build their homes? Or had he, as some others imagined, accumulated the 1000 acres of W-Hollow as kind of a sweet memory he wanted to save, like a rose pressed between the pages of the family Bible? I couldn't tell from his voice; yet I had to know.

Which was he: the accumulator with dollar signs in his eyes or the poet with remembering in his heart?

"Would you like to see this valley of yours filled with homes?" I said.

We had passed beyond the bunches of houses that had taken root along W-Hollow Road just off the county road. We were bouncing along in wilderness, nothing on either side of us but the high and dark green hills. Where the road ran, little meadows were, some in tobacco, some in meadow grass, but the little meadows ended abruptly—and there went the steep hills, keeping watch. Ahead of us, the turns and twists of the little hollow, shimmering in August green.

"No," Jesse Stuart was saying. "I wouldn't care to see all this built-up. I'd like to leave it this way. I'd like to see it held intact: a place for wildlife. I'd keep it pretty much as it is. Boy, I wish that *could* be worked! Kentucky, you know, is a state of beautiful parks. We lead just about every state in the Union in parks. Parks in Kentucky are a big industry. You can't believe it till you visit some of them. New York is the only other state that comes close, and we've passed them up. I think we even have one course at the university where they teach 'parks.' New York may have a course like that, too."

"Doesn't it bother you," I said, "to know that someday this hollow may be changed?"

"Yes," he said. I could sense the troubling in his voice. "I've worked all my life for what we've got here. I was right down here"—he waved his arm at a meadow—"working for my mother and father. I had to be at least between nine and twelve years old. That was when we lived in the house we do now, long before those rooms were added. We rented the place. We never owned land ourselves. We were sharecroppers. I looked up and there was my mother hoeing and I was hoeing and my dad was plowing. He stopped the plow above us on that very hill over there. I said, 'Some of these days I'm going to own every bit of land we've rented.' They laughed. My goodness, they laughed till they cried. Well, my mother didn't see me get the last farm. She died in 1951. My dad died in 1954—and he saw me buy the last parcel of all this."

He stopped the car, shut off the engine, and we sat in hollow silence, contemplating the putting together of the 1000-acre dream.

"Why *did* you want to buy all this?" I said.

He peered at me, puzzled. "Darned if I do really know," he said. "Maybe it was the Scotch in me or something. All I can think of is the way we all worked. I loved my parents. Maybe that's how I come to buy this. I never had too much money. Most pieces of W-Hollow were bought on a shoe-string, credit, and all. Somebody called me only the other night and said, 'The old writing paid you right down the line, didn't it?' and I said, 'Guess again. The writing never paid that well. I bought most of these parcels on what I was making, one hundred dollars a month.' Nobody wanted the pieces of land I bought. Most of them laughed at me back then for buying what I did."

"Are you still buying?" I said.

He shook his head no. Rubbing his jaw, he said, "Not any more. When I bought the farm down on the river for corn, I had to pay so high a price for it—being a river farm— that I sort of stopped buying land. I had to pay one thousand dollars an acre down there. Up here, the highest I ever paid was seventeen dollars an acre. A lot up here I got for

even less than that. That was back there when they were almost trying to give most of it away. I was making, as I said,
one hundred dollars a month. I'd sell a poem for ten dollars
or a story for twenty-five dollars and I'd put every cent of
the writing money into land. I bought forty-eight acres, one
tract that has timber on it now, for six hundred and forty-
four dollars, because they had no way to get the cut timber
to the mill. Today, it's beautiful land—and worth lots
more."

"How many separate transactions do you think you made
to acquire the thousand acres?" I said.

He pondered that a moment.

"I would say a little more than two dozen different transactions," he said. "The smallest would be less than one acre, the
oddest strip you've ever seen. I had to pay one hundred and
fifty dollars for it right there on the hilltop. Wasn't worth
the money, but I had land on the other side of it and the
sliver in between was fouling me up. So I went and bought it.
The biggest transaction, I think, was buying two hundred
and twenty-two acres for around two thousand five hundred
dollars."

"How did you get your first land?"

"It was one acre," he said. "I traded four dollars worth of
'possum hides for it. It was right over there"—he pointed
to a bit of meadow. "Now it's been improved until you
wouldn't know it. It was an awful place when I bought it. It
was when I was a boy. So it goes to show you what the
dream of a youth can be. That was some dream. . . ."

He started the car again. We moved along the hollow road
toward his home.

"Is there any cheap land left?" I said.

"No sir!" he said. "Not around here, there's not. I'll bet there's not any in Ohio, either, unless you get right down into southern Ohio along the river. You've got a few miles along there where the land might be cheap. I don't know why you Ohioans skipped that when you could have put a four-lane road along the river. That's one of the prettiest drives in the world, along the Ohio side of the river. I never could understand why Ohio never developed it."

We passed a stand of corn.

"There's something," the poet said. "The food that's here. Five generations of mine have lived in this valley and most never bought anything in the way of food from the store except salt, sugar, pepper, and things like that. Not always sugar, either. We'd sweeten with honey or sorghum. I've eaten the food in this valley and grew up to manhood on what this valley produced. All this used to be farmed; now most is meadow, I guess. We'd rent the land from the owners and eat what we raised. We had mule teams for power. We never had much level land. We farmed what level ground there was, then we farmed the sides of the hills. I used to clear hills for farming when I was a little boy. We raised corn for meal. We raised wheat and turned it into flour. We raised enough wheat one time that we could have supplied all of Greenup. We cradled it with cradles, hauled it to the barn, and thrashed it. We had an awful lot of flour here."

"And now?"

"You've got the government adjusting everything," he said. "We used to plant all the tobacco we wanted. Now we raise just so much. There'll never be another time like the time I lived when I was a boy."

We had arrived at his home. We went into the house.

Deane was off somewhere—shopping, she had said—so we made ourselves comfortable in one of the living rooms. Forgotten was the Plum-Grove-Cemetery mood. Land, and the use of it, was on the poet's mind.

"Dick," he said, "consider some of the trees we got back on one of the hills. I wish I could *give* them to somebody for firewood. That would clean up some of the forest."

I had to smile.

"Writers edit paragraphs," I said. "Farmers edit forests."

He nodded. "You're right," he said. "Let me tell you something I learned from nature. Nature is one of the best editors on the face of the earth. Consider the wind blowing through the timber. Sure, it might blow a tree down once in a while, but wind among timber is good. It prunes the trees, blowing the dead limbs out. Each year we go through and pick up dead limbs. We used to, that is, before we started using the bush-hog, one of the greatest inventions to keep the land tidy and in good shape. But sell the timber and have somebody come in and take it all out? Not on your life! They're destroyers. They would rip it all down, leaving the forest a wasteland, marked only by stumps where the forest had been."

"When was the last time you killed anything on your land?" I said.

"It was 1943," he said. "I killed squirrels."

"What was the turning point for you?" I said.

He leaned forward in his chair, peering at me as if to heap his understanding on me. "I couldn't stand to kill," he said. "I killed for two things. I killed for our table—squirrels, groundhogs, even 'possums. Mom would cook them. We didn't have enough money to buy meat. So I killed for the table and then I sold the hides, 'possum hides, too. I was always selling pelts. That's how I bought books. . . ."

The 'possum died that man may grow. The rabbit became a textbook and the squirrel became a book of sonnets.

Jesse Stuart was saying, "But I got *acquainted* with all these animals I killed and I just couldn't kill them any more. I quit killing. I thought of the day they would disappear from the face of the earth"—the last squirrel, the last 'possum —"and they're going to disappear, too, if we don't *do* something about it. W-Hollow is their only stronghold here in the county. They can always get something to eat here. Naomi Deane keeps peanut butter on bread out back of the house for the 'possums. And we keep corn out there, too."

I had seen one of them, fat and content, peering from under the shed at their kitchen door. The circle, in some way, was then complete: the 'possum had died that sonnets be written and sonnets were written that the 'possum be fed.

"We have deer around here," Jesse Stuart said. "We got them, too. We protect them. My goodness, they eat salt with our cattle and everything. But they won't stay in one place. We feed 'em and there they go, they leave."

We waited in the room of the ticking clocks for one of the clocks to finish chiming. Then the poet said, "One of my next books coming out is about a white deer and a little girl. It was turned down seven times before I found a publisher. It is one of the most beautiful things I've ever written, but they didn't want it in the East. But there's a little house doing it. They're calling it *Come to My Tomorrow Land*. The Eastern houses wouldn't take it because I wouldn't cut out some things. I tried, but couldn't, Dick. But this editor at this little publishing house did a marvelous job. He had an analytical mind. He's made my book into a little classic. They're down in Nashville. The head of the publishing house used to be director for Notre Dame. . . ."

He looked at me thoughtfully. "A lot has come out of this land, you see?" he said. "But we put most right back into it. I've done experimenting here before the United States government got around to it. I planted walnuts in sand, and in would go young sprouts, and up they would come. I was rebuilding a whole hillside with trees again. Only I had this heart attack and a boy went along with a scythe and whopped the sprouts down. He didn't know a walnut tree from a ragweed. Cut 'em all down."

The poet seemed sad about that.

I thought of W-Hollow and the W-Hollow road, the several miles back from the county road in the convoluted hollow surrounded by the hills. That morning, driving in, the valley had been wet and gray with mountain mist the sun had not burned off. I had stopped by a stand of tobacco, all stacked up in neat rows, and felt like a kid pretending. The tobacco, the way it was stacked, looked like small-scale Indian tepees. In the fog that swirled in and around them, they seemed an orderly Indian village that history had plopped down there fresh and new. But silence was everywhere, except one bird that sang. The village of the fog was silent-land; the Indians had all gone. Yes, there is much a man can dream about in W-Hollow. There's much there that triggers dreams. I told Jesse Stuart about this. He did not think I was childish. We got to talking about the road itself. It didn't go through the middle of the hollow but hung along the edge on the north side of it.

"That's because it's better on ground a little higher," Jesse

Stuart said. "You couldn't put the road in the hollow bottom itself. We flattened out some of the rises on that little road. Time was, teams stalled on some of the hilly parts of the hollow road. I'll bet we dumped a hundred wagonloads of rock in one place that was swampy, making her passable. . . ."

He fell to reflecting.

"Back in one of the cutoffs," he said, "there's a log house, on one of the prongs of the W that makes W-Hollow. It's a pretty little house, too. The stone chimney is still there. Fieldstone. Next to the house is a tree that's dying. We tried to save it, but we couldn't. We had a ladder in that tree so the chickens could roost on its limbs. We lived there awhile ourselves, you see. We had a barn and a shed and grapevines, too. My sister and I would get up on those vines and just wallow. We even had a goose come around once and lay an egg. I used to marvel at geese. All you have to do for a nest egg is put a white doorknob in the nest and the goose would lay to it. Geese just don't know any better, I guess."

He seemed sad about something.

"We worked hard, Dick. We really worked," he said. But his voice said times have changed. Work, it seems, has gone out of favor in the land. "We worked like mules," he said, "but . . ."

"And *now?*" I said.

He rubbed his chin.

"I see people who work for the C&O Railroad," he said, "driving their trucks slow because it's close to quitting time. But we don't seem to have that around here. I've got men on the place, I send them out, and I choose 'em right. They're good workers and honest ones. I never even go see what they do. I may check sometime, but the point is, I don't *have* to be there, watching over them. They know what to do. They're that kind of people. But you can't do that with the average man. These fellows here on the place are wonderful and special. Fine, *fine* people. There's not many of that kind left in the world. They know how to use an axe. They know how to swing a scythe. They're actually better now than I am, because since the heart attack I'm getting away from that. I used to do it good. There's a way to use less strokes on a scythe and get the ground cut right. How many people today would think to keep one blade of an axe sharp and the other dull so you can use the dull side for shrubbing—that's when you cut something with an axe that you can't cut with a scythe. The sharp bit of the axe is for cutting down a tree. There's much to know that people don't. Bud Adams, who works for me, paves the way for cleaning the woods by using the bush-hog. There's really a labor saver."

"What," said city me, "is a bush-hog?"

"It's got these things like a helicopter, a blade underneath that comes around and just mows through the rough stuff like it wasn't there. It's tractor-drawn. It replaces entire cutting crews. It'll cut off a whole field. When we didn't have a bush-hog we had crews with scythes, good crews of eight or nine men. Now machinery has reduced this to a few. Bud Adams goes first and paves the way. They follow, just trimming here and there, or going into places the bush-hog itself can't go. Bud will cut over against a creek real close; they'll come through and finish up. But they don't have too much to cut because Bud is a master."

"Do other people keep their land so neat?" I said.

"They could," he said, "but they don't. You saw the farms near the cemetery. If I had those places two weeks, you wouldn't recognize them as the same. The fencerows would be cleaned out. The fields would be cut off. It would be a new place entirely."

"The people have changed?"

He nodded.

"Years ago," he said, "you had people who stood for something. They were individuals. They wouldn't let it go. They weren't that kind."

"Are there any individuals like that left in this part of the country?" I said.

"All I know," the poet said, "is I won't let things go. My wife won't let things go. I've got a brother that won't let things go. I've got sisters that won't let things go. I've got some nieces and nephews that won't let things go. There's a lot of my dad in all of us. Most of us he'd trained. Our kin have built houses for themselves with their own hands. Some are college people but that makes no difference. They get satisfaction doing and building with their hands. My kin can plumb and wire and farm and everything."

"It's a matter of upbringing," I said.

He agreed. "My goodness, yes," he said. "There's an old saying back in school that is as true as it can be: an idle room is the devil's workshop. When students are idle, it's the devil's workshop. The same goes for the young today."

"But," I said, "isn't the opposite just 'make-work' and rather empty at times?"

"I suppose," he said. "But I'd rather have them on make-work than doing nothing. If there's nothing for people to do, I'd think up programs for them. I thought up a program for the whole country years ago. It had to do with cleaning up the countrysides. I've even written in *Reader's Digest* about this. Conservation of the soil! All of it! I've been interested for thirty years in taking care of wildlife and preserving it. Sometimes Naomi Deane and I will go along the hollow road, clear to the county road, picking up cans and bottles that litter there. It makes a difference. It makes the hollow beautiful. I'm glad this is beginning to interest the rest of the country, too. Everybody's waking up, worrying about pollution. Why, it's beginning to make a difference. Other countries don't have the pollution we have here. Germany doesn't have it. France doesn't have it. England, Scotland, Ireland —none of those countries have it. Egypt doesn't have it. Greece doesn't have it. I've been to all these places and I *know*. They just don't have it. I don't know how they do it."

We talked awhile of Louis Bromfield and Malabar. Both Bromfield and Stuart, as passionate custodians of the land, once seemed far ahead of their time. Now the world is catching up a little.

He ached to give me a tour of his 1000 acres, but I suggested waiting a day or so. I wanted to know him as a person better first. He agreed but with polite reluctance. W-Hollow was his world; he wanted to let others wonder at the beauty of it.

"I'll show you the side of a hill that we had in corn when I was a boy," he said. "It's so steep you won't believe it. We had another side of a hill in wheat and it was just as slanty. Today it's all in timber, but I would like for you to see it."

"I'd like to see places where your dad actually filled in gullies, smoothing them out," I said.

"I'll show you that, too," he said. "You won't even be able to tell where the gullies were! My dad made his fifty rented acres into the prettiest place."

CARL A. RUDISILL LIBRARY
LENOIR RHYNE COLLEGE

"Is Bud Adams much like your dad?" I said.

"A lot," Jesse Stuart agreed. "They've both got good ideas about things. My dad was a very positive man. If my dad went through the woods and saw where somebody had skinned a tree, taking the bark off with an axe or hatchet or blade, for no good reason at all, my dad would try to track them down. He would try to find out who did it. If he'd find a fire that wasn't put out, he would never stop till he found out who left it. My dad wouldn't take no for an answer. And he wouldn't even have as much as an air gun on the place. Wouldn't let anybody walk across his place carrying any kind of gun."

"Did he have many problems that way?" I said.

Jesse Stuart agreed.

"He did," said the poet, "but he took care of them."

I asked him about something I'd noticed.

"I saw all the 'No Trespassing' signs on either side of the hollow road."

"And 'No Hunting' signs, too," Jesse Stuart added. "I've got 'No Hunting' signs just about everywhere. I bought another dozen of them in Ashland last night."

"But do people abide by them?"

"A lot of people will," he said. "Now and then, somebody will slip in. The other day, down here, one of them slipped by without my noticing. But when he came back down the road, out of the hollow, there I was, standing and waiting for him. I got him, too. I even went and got a warrant for him because I knew him. He works over in Ashland. But he claimed he never saw the sign, so I let him go."

"Why?" I asked.

Jesse Stuart made a helpless motion.

"Well," he said, "I honestly don't believe he did see the 'No Trespassing' sign. But boy, if I knew he had seen it and had ignored it, I think I might have worked him over. But you see, I don't believe the fellow saw it. Why would he lie to me? He comes from one of the finest families in the county, he works hard every day, so I believed him. On the other hand, there are many I wouldn't believe. But his family is all right. There was never a criminal among them. Most were schoolteachers and business people—good workers, every one of them. So I just got to thinking about it. They're all good friends of mine. So I told this fellow that. I said to him, 'How in the world could you ever get in here and hunt on me without permission? You're supposed to have the permission of the owner. Even if the signs weren't there, regardless of the signs, that's the law.' I had him, see? He hadn't done it. He hadn't asked permission. But he's got a good job in Ashland. I could have called up and maybe got him fired for something like this. But I know his people. So I didn't."

"Do people picnic on your land?" I said.

He pondered this.

"Some do," he said, "and that's all right. We let them come. They can come as long as they don't bring guns with them. They can enjoy the nature here. I'm proud to share it with them. They can enjoy the beauty here just so they don't set fires. Let them enjoy the wind and the trees and the flowers. But we don't want guns. And we don't want fires that could destroy all this. And I mean it."

W-Hollow is back a ways from civilization and the Greenup fire department. By the time the volunteers arrived, a little fire could have been wind-whipped into a massive one, laying waste to hills and hills of timber.

"Have you ever had a fire on your place?" I said.

Even the thought of it troubled him. I could tell by his voice.

"Oh, my Lord, yes," he said. "People have got out here and fought fires. We've had a whole high school turn out to fight 'em. We had a fire right here in this hollow where the house is. Somebody dropped a match and the fire blazed, just blazed up the hill like the trees had sucked it. The meadow was so dry, the electric power poles blazed. We carried water and put it out. I wasn't supposed to be out, doing that, but I went out with a boy helping me and we fought that one. We raked a ring on one end down there by the steep bank and stopped it. But we had to do it. It would have ruined the whole hollow if we hadn't done it."

"Did it last long?" I said.

"Not very long. We got it stopped before it had climbed midway up the hill. That one was mean. It could have burned this whole country up. There's an awful lot of area in W-Hollow that hasn't been burned off. We keep it protected and other people have protected it for us. Back along the ridge line, up there on the hill behind the house, is our fire break. We had a fire up there one time and there was no braking it. We just couldn't get it turned off. We managed to save at least part of the woods, though. Oh, you should have seen the smoke boiling up and the flames boiling up. We had to rebuild a mile of fence because of one fire up there. Bud Adams had plowed a fire lane right along the fencerow with the tractor, knocking fences over and everything, but there was no way else to stop it. It was an awful fire. We couldn't get enough men. They're paid here to fight fires.

They got a fire company up here, too, but we didn't used to have that. Back then it was almost every man for himself, only his neighbors helped. They'd get fires on their side we would help put out and they would help put out the fires we got over here. We didn't have any telephones back then, either. We were always on the watch, like on duty, waiting for a fire to start. But we've probably had less fires back here than anywhere because we're so strict about it. We try to get to 'em before they get out of hand. Now that we have telephones and a regular fire warden in the county, things are easier. But you'll find most neighbors here fighting the fire before help arrives from Greenup. All of us know how to fight fires. We have to.

"We build backfires. That's a big way to do it. And to prevent fires, you have your farm fixed up, you build fire lanes. I'll show you some when we take a trip around W-Hollow. Cutting a fire off is the important thing. It could ruin us if we didn't have fire lanes. We've got all kinds of places on W-Hollow so tractors with blades can go fight the fires. We built the lanes special, just for that. Why, this house here could go like tinder. That's the reason we have a non-burnable roof on it. If anything flaming blew through the sky and hit the house, the roof wouldn't catch. The shingles on the side are nonflammable—almost."

"What about fires when you were a boy?"

"The most dangerous you've ever seen!" Jesse Stuart said. "I've seen them plow till the horse fell over. I've seen a fire once blow from the top of this hill right here clean across the open space of the valley to that hill over there. Then they plowed at it till the horse fell, but they finally got the fire stopped. Yes, that old horse worked till it up and keeled over. This horse wasn't trained to get too close to the heat and that was it."

"What about when you and your wife leave W-Hollow, say, and go to Europe?" I said. "Who watches the place?"

"There's always someone living in the house when we're away," he said. "Used to be, my parents would come along and check it every day. The Adams family do it for us now."

"And vandalism?"

I had the city fear of an apartment dweller. The emptiness of the land still made me cautious.

Jesse Stuart shrugged. "We don't have much vandalism in the area," he said. "It's almost nil. There was a little vandalism happened over at the end of the road where my niece moved in. She was away at school, teaching, and he was working, and somebody went in and hauled off their television. Some other stuff, too: an old antique gun, a lamp, and things of that nature. That's the only vandalism I've heard of here. We haven't had any breaking-and-enterings, either. My brother-in-law doesn't even lock his door when he goes out. He goes to work at Ashland Oil and Refining Company and my sister teaches school. They never lock up. Why? Because there's only two ways out of the hollow. All you have to do is block off both exits to the county roads and you got 'em. There's no way to lug a television over the ridge. . . ."

I said nothing.

How can you ask a dreamer how long the dream will last?

SEVEN

"LADY ASTOR," Jesse Stuart announced, "was a honey!"

He stood before one of the bookcases in one of the living rooms. He was seeking a copy of *Tales from the Plum Grove Hills*. I sat across the room, waiting. I got the biggest kick out of him. He never did anything halfway. He was the perfect *doer*. The conversation had begun on the subject of dust jackets for books. It did not linger there. Jesse Stuart wanted to show me the dust jacket for the book he sought. "Most beautifully designed jacket of any book I've ever written," he had said. "An Italian did it. Balances of red and black and all. The colors are out of this world. Italians are great artists, you know. They're great builders, too. Look at the Roman Empire. The Italians had done the stone work for it. They've done it for Spain. They've done it for Egypt. They've done it for England. They've done it for Germany. And they've done it for France. In my estimation, they're a great artisan race and great workers. We underestimate them. Everybody jokes about the Italians. They shouldn't."

Then he had gone to the bookshelf.

"Have you traveled in all the countries you'd like to visit?" I had said.

"Most," he had said. Then, out of the blue, he called Lady Astor a honey.

Forgotten was the book jacket. He came back across the room to sit beside me. *The Connecticut Yankee in King Arthur's Court*—change that to read the Kentucky poet, but keep the red, white, and blue in there strong, please—was wound up on the idea of England and the rest.

"I stayed with Lady Astor, at her house, for two weeks," he said. "I was over there in 1937 on this Guggenheim Fellowship. I think I was the first Kentuckian to get that kind of fellowship, but maybe I wasn't. If I wasn't, I was awful close to being first. I was twenty-nine years old at the time. Well, I went over there to England. She heard about me being there, a young American author on a fellowship, so she sent for me. As I said, I stayed there at Five St. James Square two weeks, which was her place. I had the tiniest key for the biggest door I ever saw. She was a fine lady. Her relatives were kin of mine from Virginia. We found that out later, though. She was just being nice to a poor writer. That's the way she was. I never saw Winston Churchill when I was there, but Lady Astor said he came around a lot. And one time she asked me what I missed most in England and I told her I missed good cigars, and she said, 'Well, I'll give you a couple that I'll bet will be good ones.' She went and brought me some cigars that Winston Churchill had left."

"Were they good?"

"Oh my goodness, yes," said Jesse Stuart. He rubbed his hands with enthusiasm. "I'll bet they cost every bit of a dollar apiece. He'd order them from someplace. I really enjoyed smoking them."

And enjoyed wandering about London, feeling his way

through fog; listening to the boom of Big Ben in the unseen misty tower; hearing the creak of rigging on unseen boats on the unseen Thames; overhearing the thousand cockney accents; and gathering in pubs and Piccadilly on wet and foggy nights, mixing and mingling with other fledgling poets with dialects from Scotland and Ireland and England and Wales. None of them could understand how Jesse Stuart managed to be staying at Lady Astor's. They were properly impressed.

So was I.

I was about to say so when Deane entered the room.

"Boys," she said, "what would you like to drink with your lunch? I've fixed a cheese soufflé."

"Would you like a beer, Dick?" Jesse said to me.

"For beer lovers," said Deane, "we have Michelob."

We adjourned to the kitchen and sat around the table.

"I like a little beer sometimes with my cheese," said the poet, digging in. "But it puts weight on me. I'm trying to cut down. But I sure can drink beer. I did it in Germany. Can't stand their coffee so I *had* to drink something. You know what I used to have for breakfast on those trains in Germany? Either a hot dog or a cheese sandwich—and a beer. Can you imagine that? But France, though, has the best cooking in the world. Everywhere! You go out on a farm some out-of-the-way place and the food is wonderful. Those French people know how to cook."

"Was your mother a good cook?" I said.

"She wasn't," he said, peering at me. "Not many of my relatives are. But I'll tell you something. The English aren't good with foods, either, compared to other countries over there. The English don't live to eat; they're plain-food people. The Scots are the same and so are the Irish. But you get over to France and Italy and you get spicy foods. You get good food in Greece. In Denmark the goulash is excellent. But higher up in the Scandinavian countries, it's boiled potatoes and lots of fish, fixed lots of different ways."

Deane poured the coffee for us.

"They're dry up there, too," Jesse Stuart went on. "Oslo is a city as big as Louisville but it's got only three places that sell spirits. And at the time they led the world in education. In Louisville you can buy a drink nearly everywhere—and at the time Kentucky was one of the lowest states in the country as far as education was concerned. I gave a talk down in Louisville one time and told them that!"

Deane's soufflé was perfection.

"Another thing about Europe," said Jesse Stuart, tackling the soufflé, "they drink but you never see a drunk. I believe I saw *one* man staggering. That was in Venice. It was so unusual, everybody was giving him looks. And I saw one staggering in Switzerland. Everybody was giving him looks, too. They're civilized over there, Dick. In America you see people walking down sidewalks and they got toothpicks in their mouths. Over there, you don't see that."

"But I don't remember seeing many drunks on the streets of this country," I said, "except places like Skid Row."

He nodded. "But on special days down here," he said, "these Kentuckians can get too much. It's more in the country than in the towns. In the country, they get lit up. When they celebrate, they celebrate all the way. Some around here don't figure it's a celebration unless they get too much to drink and have a fistfight. It happens sometimes up in Ashland. It happens in Portsmouth across the river. Drinking is all right if you handle it right. Why, I've sat in there and

(Top) Listing a little but still standing is the house in Greenup County, Kentrucky, where Jesse Stuart was born August 8, 1907. (Bottom) Left to right: Jesse's father, friend Gus McAbier, and the young Jesse Stuart, already nearly a head taller than his dad.

(Above) Twenty-one good men and true pose for the annual Glee Club picture at Lincoln Memorial University with their music director, Professor Gaw. Jesse, second from the left in the row of seated singers, hitchhiked to the university to begin his college education, and thus perhaps started the trend which is still going strong in the '70's.

(At top, right) The one-room school in Greenup, Kentucky, where Jesse for a year taught all pupils all subjects in Grades 1 through 8 before he went off to Vanderbilt University for a year of graduate study.

(Bottom, right) Jesse Stuart, twenty-four, takes a rest on his way to the now-defunct Riverton, Kentucky, post office to mail off the collection of poems which was to be published as *Man with a Bull-Tongue Plow*. The picture, taken by his fifteen-year-old brother, shows a glimpse of the land Jesse so often plowed with the help of the family's trusty mules.

(At top, left) Sheep, like cattle, deer and a good many other animals, have never heard of salt-free diets. A 1938 cameraman pictured Jesse administering their daily ration to part of his flock in the pastures of the Stuart farm.

(At bottom, left) Jesse was in his early twenties when this picture of him was made, as he says, "plowing right up among the clouds." Hot work for man and mule, and perhaps for the photographer as well. At any rate, our plower says it's the only such picture ever taken of him.

(Above) Proof that you don't have to be a Walker Evans or own a Hasselblad to turn film into poetry is provided by this shot of a plowman on the crest of one of the scores of steep hills which are part of the W-Hollow landscape. Long since forgotten is the name of the photographer who held the Brownie camera—more's the pity.

(At left) What would a picture spread be without a close look at the teacher who writes (or writer who teaches) with his young wife and their baby daughter? Jesse and Deane "sat" for a formal portrait with infant Jane, who was born in Ashland, Ohio, August 20, 1942.

(Above) Lt. (jg) Jesse Stuart, like a great many young Americans, served in the Navy during World War II. In off-duty hours he followed the course of many a serviceman and his family and toured the high spots of the Nation's capital. Here he relaxes with Jane and Deane on the lawn outside a Washington hive of industry.

(At left) Jesse and Jane at Plum Grove Cemetery near W-Hollow. The poet's mother and father, one of his grandfathers, and countless friends are buried in this country resting place. Jesse's own plot is on the exact spot where, as a boy, he sat in the back row of the one-room school and watched the changing seasons through the window nearest his desk.

(At right) A prime gourd crop attracts Jesse's eye during a warm summer early in the Stuart's married life. Deane's eyes are perhaps looking ahead to autumn-ripening pumpkins and pie.

(Above) Jesse's father mined coal and to bring it out of the diggings he laid a roadbed, put down track, and built his own rolling stock. What helped a miner earn a living here provides a joy ride for Jane Stuart and a visiting niece of Jesse and Deane, here called on to provide motive power.

(At right) Dogs were as much a part of Kentucky farm life as sheep, cattle, hogs and crops. Here is Jesse in 1946 with Terry-B, a favorite pet.

(At top, left) The houses you live in, work in, worship in play a big part in your life if you aren't a city dweller in a multi-story apartment which is the exact duplicate of the building next door. The roots of such a bond perhaps lie in the fact that you helped build it and know what love and labor went into every beam and shingle and piece of siding. Here is the cabin into which Jesse and Deane moved some time after they were married. It was their first "home of your own," with a spanking new addition put on by Jesse.

(Bottom, left) In a house which other people share, there are often distractions which make it difficult for a writer to do his best work undisturbed. Jesse Stuart found a ready answer to the problem in this bunkhouse, long a fixture of the farm, situated behind the main house. Here he wrote as he pleased, bothered by nothing more than familiar country sounds.

(Above) The Pine Grove Church was and is an integral part of Plum Grove Cemetery, source of inspiration and solace to Jesse over the years. If it looks a little bare, try to imagine its crude but fine plank and weatherboard construction. A new church has replaced this one, but the congregation couldn't bear to leave the beautiful wood behind, and incorporated much of it in the new structure.

EARL PALMER PHOTO

(Above) At home and proud of it, the young Stuarts. It must have taken almost as much work to get the massive stone slab on which they're standing put down in place as it did to build the house.

(Bottom, left) Wife, friend, gentle critic, Deane often goes over Jesse's work before it is sent off to a publisher. Together they look at the draft of a new manuscript as they sit at the kitchen table.

FRANK ROSS PHOTO

The book on his knee forgotten for the moment, Jesse sits in the warm summer sun, thinking, musing, or lost in the dreams which just being in W-Hollow foster.

COURIER-JOURNAL AND LOUISVILLE TIMES PHOTO

(Above) There are two living rooms in the Stuart's present house in the Hollow. This one is called simply "living room number one." Like its counterpart, it has been lovingly furnished by Deane with the kind of chairs and tables and fireplace tools and rugs which were, many years ago, a heritage in Kentucky homes but are now increasingly hard to find. (At top, right) In 1955 Jesse Stuart suffered a massive heart attack just after he had completed a lecture in a Kentucky college auditorium. He spent the year of his recovery in his bedroom at W-Hollow, where you see him here. He began a vigil over the tiny world seen through his window: winter birds, morning mist, a three-legged possum. (At bottom, right) When it appeared that Stuart would indeed recover from his near-fatal coronary, he was allowed limited exercise and a chance to get outdoors again. But visitors were a drain on his strength and had to be barred—a matter perhaps as hard for a gregarious man to adjust to as inactivity.

FRANK ROSS PHOTO

FRANK ROSS PHOTO

FRANK ROSS PHOTO

(Top) Jesse tends to the day's news while Jane and Deane tend the flower garden bordering the path to the front door. (Bottom) W-Hollow today. Jane and Dean weave daisy chains while Jesse has eyes in the back of his head for grandson Conrad Stuart.

watched the Cincinnati Redlegs on television and I'd be sipping Scotch. A few extra sips and I just got to go to bed. I'm not really a drinking man, I suppose. I never had whisky in my mouth till I was in my fifties. Was always a teetotaler. Never drank anything but wine in France and beer in Germany because there I drank it instead of water. After I had my heart attack, the doctor put me on Scotch. That's how come I drink it now. It relaxes me, makes me sleep. I don't smoke any more, you see. Smoking used to relax me good. But since I don't, I take Scotch. It's medicinal. A couple jiggers on a piece of ice, a little water, and that'll put me to bed!"

"You've traveled a lot?" I said.

"My goodness, yes," Jesse Stuart said. "We've traveled considerably. We've been to every state in the Union but Alaska. If we live, we plan to touch there, too. I don't know how many times I've been in some states, but I've been in most of them more than once. I've been to Hawaii two or three times. Once when it was raining cats and dogs in Dakar, the capital of Senegal on the West African coast, Naomi Deane and I sat around listening to the noise the rain made and we figured up how many countries we *had* been in. I've been to seventy-five of 'em and Naomi Deane has been to fifty. We've been in some several times, like Italy and Greece. We actually lived in Greece and Egypt. In figuring up, we found I'd been in and out of Lebanon sixteen times and she'd been in and out of there seventeen times."

"Why this urge to travel?" I said.

He sat, sifting his thoughts.

"Well," he said at last, "I like a break from my land and what I'm doing. And I want to see the world, Dick. It's a big place. I like to see other people and what's going on. I feel as if out there is part of me, too. I have this feeling for W-Hollow but I have this feeling for all the rest. But here is home. I am part of these hills and hollows, this land; and this is the land that made me. Here," he concluded almost gently, "is my spot on earth. Right here . . ."

"Why don't you boys go back in the living room," Deane suggested. "You'll be more comfortable there."

We adjourned to the living room. The poet was still preoccupied by thoughts of his native land and how, it seemed, the people in it lacked the values their ancestors once had. He settled himself in a lounge chair, rubbed his hands together, and looked at me, gazing the gaze of a seeker.

"But there's not much competition left here any more," he said. "We won't be what we have been if competition dies. That's what has deadened socialist countries. They're dead. They're gone. Look at Russia. Look at all the other countries. I visited them and *know*. I've been around the world, Dick. All the youngsters out there"—he waved to indicate millions of children beyond our border—"want to come to this country. Over there, when they go to school, you can't drive them away. They love it. But here . . ."

He did not say. It did not need the saying.

In 1960 Jesse Stuart took his wife and daughter to Cairo, Egypt, where he was teaching as visiting professor at the American University. Deane taught second grade in a private American School—for children of the diplomats at Maadi, a Cairo suburb. Jane, their daughter, took her freshman year at college at the American University there. While in that part of the world, they traveled through the Holy Land, Jordan, Syria, and Lebanon; and before returning to this country they went just about everywhere in Europe that was available. In 1962, our State Department sent the poet around the world on a lecture tour. The department's only request was, "Please don't lose your temper." The poet and his wife, whose transportation he paid himself, traveled 2500 miles by plane, train, and jeep in Iran alone! While in Iran, he lectured in Teheran, Meshed, Shiraz, and Esfahan. In only two countries—Iran and Korea—did Jesse Stuart speak through an interpreter. In Egypt, Greece, Lebanon, West Pakistan, East Pakistan, the Philippines, and the Republic of Free China (on Formosa) they heard his Kentucky accent unvarnished. In 1966, the poet and his wife spent the summer in Athens, Greece, where Jane attended school. In 1968, the Jesse Stuarts went back to Africa and Europe again to give it the Kentucky once-over. In 1969 they visited Europe again and Africa. When Jesse Stuart speaks of other countries, he knows whereof he speaks.

"Dick," he said, leaning forward, "I battled Communists around the world. They had their questions for me. I had my questions for them. I could always tell who was the leftist. One question a leftist always asks over there is 'Why are Americans so contemptible?' Then they go on to other set questions, like what about our competition, like how we robbed the rest of the world, and like how we got everything ourselves. They'd start on me and I'd say, 'Now I'll tell you how we're robbing the world and about our competition. Do you know that six percent of our people'—and this was true at the time—'live on farms but raise enough food to feed 200 million people?' I tell them about the grain we'd stored and how we feed other countries by just giving it to them. That's true, too. When I was teaching in Egypt they said if it hadn't been for the United States, they would have starved. Russia built a dam for them, but we put food in their bellies with the wheat we gave 'em. And I would tell the leftists how come we could do this with six percent of our people, whereas in Russia fifty-two percent can't raise enough food for people and fodder for cattle. Those were Khrushchev's own words I'd give back to them. I'd really light into them. They'd tell me we had the best land and I'd tell them no. What about the land around the Black Sea? That's beautiful soil there. Russia honestly has some of the finest land in the world, but what good is it doing them? As for competition, I would tell 'em, 'We have the machinery and the know-how and do you know who got it for us? There's some Russians on our farms. We've got Germans on them. We've got Danes on them. We've got people from all over the world farming in the United States.' They couldn't answer me and they'd want to slip away, but I wouldn't let them. I had them good. My goodness, I battled them everywhere I went."

He leaned back, rubbed his crew cut, and said: "The Koreans were wonderful, just wonderful. *Pro* United States. The Philippines would have liked to have belonged to us. We didn't give them the right to vote, though. When we let Hawaii vote, it voted itself right into this country. The Philippines would have done the same thing, but you know why we didn't give them the chance? Too far out there. They're Asians, you know. But what a wonderful country they have."

"What country would you like to revisit?" I said.

He didn't hesitate.

"Greece," he said. "I just love Greece. I'd like Asia, if they'd get out of that damn war and behave themselves. That thing's going on and on, isn't it? I liked Egypt and the Egyp-

tians, too. They are the finest students. There were a lot of
Greeks among them when I was there. Greeks—and Moslem girls. They're great students. Simply out of this world.
You don't have any problems *morally* with Moslem girls. Im-
morality is punishable by death among the Moslem people."

"But do they still do that?" I said.

"Oh my goodness, yes," he said. "It happened twice on the
Gaza strip. They did it in Iran. I have a paper somewhere
around the house here that has a story of that in it. But
you've never seen any girls like that anywhere else. Now,
though, they're getting away from wearing veils. When they
came to school, they were so bright!"

"Is there a morality problem here, then?" I said.

"Yes," he said. "It *is* a problem. It is in schools here. We
don't have good morals in some places in this country. Let's
not kid ourselves. When boys can go into girls' dormitories
and girls can go into boys' dormitories, you just know there's
something going on somewhere. Everyone goes around saying sex should be free. Not everyone, but it's a *loud* minority
that goes around saying it. Some of these girls in this country
will drift from group to group—and the boys will, too.
They come from good homes but they get mixed up. I know
case after case of that. The daughter of one of my former students, she was in the genius bracket, but she went to France
on some kind of scholarship, got mixed up morally, came
back to this country, and lost her mind. She was a real mental
for awhile. She's just now coming out of it. That was several
years ago. That's the effect this stuff has on some of these
sensitive girls."

"What's the answer?" I said.

He rubbed his chin and peered at me.

"Homes and teachers and ministers," he said. "Or rabbis. I believe the Jews, in the more religious homes, have close and tight homes the way the Moslem girls had. They had tight homes. There are many things similar between the Jews and the Moslems. That's one of them. Course, most of the Moslems came from Jewish stock. But they have to go by fire and sword. Mohammed started their religion. It is the only religion built up by fire and sword. They killed one another or gouged their eyes out if they didn't join. That's how they got Moslems. Do you know how many Moslems there *are* in the world today? Five hundred million! It's one of the most devout religions we got. They pray five times a day. But they're changing a little. When they come over here, they don't pray so much. Back there, they sure do."

"Some of the Egyptians you taught," I said, "must have been the children of the Egyptian military families. How did you reach them?"

"I reached 'em all, Moslems *and* Christians alike," Jesse Stuart said. "I planted ideas in 'em, just planted the seeds. Everything in our little school paper over there was censored. We couldn't put out anything that wasn't censored. When Naomi Deane and I left Cairo, for instance, we had to report to the police where we were going and we had to report the minute we got back. My goodness, but they were childish and dictatorial. On the other hand, maybe we have too much freedom here to appreciate any of it. If those Egyptians came over here where real freedom was, they'd go hog-wild."

We paused to let one of the many clocks chime out the hour in the hollow.

"Weren't you telling me," I said, "that kids would wait

outside the schools to get in, waiting for someone to die so there would be room for them?"

"Yes!" he said. "They did that in Pakistan and they did that in Egypt. Egyptian schools had high walls around them to keep them out. But you can't keep them out in Egypt. They're all aching to go to school and learn. I got in there with ideas about schoolteaching but the authorities said they didn't have enough buildings. I said, 'Teach 'em in barns! You're losing people because you're not giving them an education. Give them an education. Teach everybody!' Didn't I teach my first high school in a barn? I sure did. There were fourteen students in that barn. Some had never even seen a picture show. Rural students, but smart. Well, these kids in Egypt are smart, too. They love American teachers. They loved Naomi Deane. Those girls would sit down by her and talk to her. Those little Moslem girls just loved her. They talked to her about her fair skin. About everything. With their olive complexions, they're beautiful people over there —all of them. Finest-looking people I've ever seen. Some of those Moslem girls were beauties. We looked upon them as beautiful. They looked upon us as beautiful. It's a funny world, isn't it?"

"Suppose," I said, "you took kids from this country and transplanted them over there for one year of high school. Would it do the American kids any good?"

"Sure," he said, "it would do them a lot of good. They'd learn to appreciate what we're giving them here on a silver platter. But you'd have to have guards around to protect them. There's much they wouldn't understand. You see, the Moslem boy is never permitted to date a girl. His marriage is

arranged for him. So the Moslem girls were chaperoned at
our school. They're not let free. They're protected in school
as well as to and from. Over here, our high school girl is free
to talk with everyone. She would sure have problems doing
that over there."

One thing troubled me. "How," I said, "did you establish
true communication right off with your classes?"

"Nothing to it," he said. "These older ones there are wise
psychologically. You got to know the way their minds work.
Ask them questions and they sit there, not answering you.
They just sit there silent. But you reach 'em. You reach 'em.
The trouble is, they had to walk a tightrope at that university. They did and we teachers did. It was our outpost there,
not for spying, but for reaching people with love."

"Were you there under Nasser?"

"Saw him nearly every day, Dick. His office was in the
National Building across from the university. I could see
from my window right into his office. And I'd see him riding
around, too, all the time waving to people, but he always had
people around him like a coat. They would have had to shoot
some of his people on the rim before they shot him. He *was*
hit twice. But don't we have the same things here? Look at
the Presidents we've had killed or shot at. There have been
several plots on Nixon. Dick, I truly don't know how you
can continue to get men to sacrifice for public office, here or
anywhere. . . ."

We spent a half hour talking about the violence of the
world. In the hollow violence seemed far away. But we could
sense its dark presence. It was in the hawk that circled its
prey. It was in the way the rabbit ran.

"They ought to," said Jesse Stuart, "get these ocean liners running again. Airplane hijacking has got so bad it scares me. And boy, look how I've ridden planes. I've been in the big ones and the small ones. I started flying in the days of barnstorming. I liked the DC-3s. But trains—trains are what I like best."

"Traveling is fun?"

"Yes, but some of the countries aren't any more," he said. "And I'd hate to fly because of the hijacking. Force ought to be answered with force. You can't reason with some of these people. They don't know what logic is. Everybody overseas acts like this country is a pushover, but I tell you, it *isn't*. We've got everything and they know it. When I first went over there in 1937 they'd always find out whether I was an American or not before they started knocking England. England was the country they knocked back then. Now it's the United States they knock."

"Do you think France will ever become a major power again?" I said.

"No," Jesse Stuart said, "and I don't think they want to be. I wish France *was* a power. I wouldn't care if Germany was a power—if they'd behave themselves."

"Germany is diverse now," I said, thinking of the division of Berlin which saddened me.

"If both Germanies could be joined back up again," said the poet, "it would be good. I'd like to see Germany put back together. They may never get another Hitler. There's not that worry. To have a Hitler is terrible for *any* country. Look at the Hitlers in the Near and Middle East. Look at all the Hitlers over there!"

"By the same token," I said, "we'll probably never get another Roosevelt because we've geared the Presidency against it: two terms only."

"Yes, we've geared the United States that way, Dick. In Nasser, you had a different kind of dictator. Did you know that Nasser couldn't stand the sight of blood? He wasn't a killer. He was a rabble-rouser."

"And opportunist?"

Jesse Stuart agreed.

"*And* opportunist," he said. "He played one country against another. He got what *he* wanted by doing it. He played the United States against Russia. Even if you live among those people, you won't truly figure them out completely. There are certain Egyptians you'll like. Some are fine people. Most of them are, in fact. There's something *ancient* about that country that makes you love it. Naomi Deane and I did. We love antiques. Anything over there that isn't a thousand years old isn't an antique. We bought this little stone head in Thebes—that's now Tunisia—where they were excavating an old city. There's no end to what's being excavated over there. We paid about three dollars for that vase. It's at least five thousand years old. It goes back to the Phoenecians. It's from one of their old buildings or something."

He fondled the antique, gazing at it, as if plumbing its stone memory.

"Over here," he said, "we gloat about history, but we really don't have any. We go back to Daniel Boone. That's not far. But in Egypt there's no history for another reason. You don't read about it. You don't study it. You're in it, surrounded by it. You see ancient gods still up on the walls. You see the pyramids. Nothing has been destroyed. It's right there where it has been for ages. A boy visited us here once from Egypt. The lady who brought him said we live in an old town here because it goes back to 1791. He only smiled. He had lived in the shadow of the pyramids which were forty-nine hundred years old by then. He was very polite. He only smiled and said, 'Yes ma'am.' And when he got away, he laughed. He had to."

"Do you get this sense of history in Greece or Italy?" I said.

He set the stone head aside.

"In Greece, you do," he said. "It's that old. Look how far back the Acropolis goes—300 or 500 B.C. Everything is old around the Mediterranean. That's where civilization started. One of the things that started it was power on the Nile River. You don't have to have a gasoline engine because the wind blows only one way, which is down through Africa. The wind blows you up the Nile River. The current brings you back down again. And look at the fertility! The soil is ninety-two feet deep over there. They boast of numbers in Egypt. They boast they have thirty million people. Well, it's great to have thirty million people but what about taking *care* of them? You can't get around the streets of Cairo without running into beggars. Most are children. I thought it was the worst I had seen. Then I saw Ethiopia. *That* was the worst I'd seen. It has more beggars than any African nation! They beg from every foreigner who comes along. God only knows how they survive. They could do it on forty cents a day, but that's a big wage. If you give one of the beggars a dime, *that* is big money to him."

"Do any of the beggar children of Egypt have any ambition?" I said.

He shook his head with melancholy.

"If they had schools, yes," he said. "There's a lot of them with ambition, but what good does it do 'em? They're always getting propaganda thrown at them. Everywhere they move, more propaganda."

"They never, then, see ultimate truths or reality?" I said.

"A few, Dick. It's mostly the Christians there that do. It's not like your Anglo-Saxon breed of Christian, though. Look what a people *they* were! And they are a dangerous people. They'll stand up, one against four, and fight. You can't get anybody to fight in Egypt unless it's a gang fight. You never see two men stand up and fight the way they do here. When I saw fighting among the Muslims, it was a gang fight. They're awkward, really. They don't know how to fight with their fists. My goodness, they are the most awkward people trying to fight that I ever saw!"

"Was that why they lost the Six-day War?" I said.

"Those Jews really fight, don't they?" he said, peering at me. "Boy, don't think they won't. They had that old one-eyed general. They're the fighters. The desert people never were. There was one exception when Lawrence of Arabia got the Arabs organised. He pulled out his pistol and shot people warring against one another. He said, 'Now come together like brothers. Let's fight.' They really went after the Turks. . . ."

Deane entered the room. She settled beside her husband.

"Have you ever considered living other places?" I said.

"There are a lot of places I would like to live," the poet said. "I'd like to have a home and live awhile in southern Greece. I just love it down there. I'd get away from all that olive-oil cooking, though. That olive-oil cooking bothers me.

And I'd like to live awhile in England. Perhaps in Kent. I love Kent. And I'd like to live in Manila. I wouldn't mind living in Korea for awhile and in Free China. I've seen all sorts of places I'd love to live—for awhile. There are places in America, too. I'd like to live along the white sand beaches somewhere between New Orleans and Mississippi. Isn't the coast beautiful along there with those big stands of pines and all that white sand? I'd like to live for a summer in New England, somewhere along the coast. I'd like to live one summer in Nova Scotia, *Evangeline* country. It's beautiful there and not as cold as you would imagine. The Gulf Current sweeps around there, so it's not as cold as Maine. A fellow who lives here in Greenup spent three weeks there and he said it wasn't. Oh, I'd like to live so many places. Egypt was fine. We lived right on the Nile River. From the portico of our apartment I could have thrown a baseball across it. If the government was stable, Egypt would be a fine place to live."

"Would it be cheaper for a writer to live outside the United States?" I said.

"Well," said Jesse Stuart, "it certainly would be cheaper to live in Egypt. But if I lived there, I would get away from what I'm writing. What I've done here is try to portray this place"—he waved to indicate the hollow and all its people and moods—"with stories and poems. But when I was in Egypt I kept a journal. I kept a journal in Greece, too. I wrote on those countries while I was there in 'em. But the journals have never been published. One has sixteen hundred pages in it: three hundred on Greece, three hundred on Africa, and so on.

"Now this is an odd thing. I used to go up to the Parthenon—they called it the 'Rock'—where eight hundred thousand people go every year. Well, they tramped the ground down around it, all but one place, and there a dandelion had survived. I looked at the Parthenon, wondering how I would write it. It has been written a thousand different ways. So you know what I did: I just let the dandelion tell the story."

He paused, pleased with himself, as we were pleased with him, too.

Then, gently, he added: "You know, Dick, we started there at the Parthenon, you and me and all of us. This country and all of us in it started at the Rock. All Europe started there. The whole Western world started there. We started with Socrates and a bunch of them other Greeks. That's where we started. . . ."

He sat, rubbing his hands, and nodding his head. The hollow was no longer there. He was standing beside the Parthenon, looking with wonder at Socrates.

EIGHT

"YOU ought to go up and talk to Bud Adams," Jesse Stuart had said. "He'll tell you how things are."

So I went up the hollow to talk to Bud Adams.

Mr. Adams and his wife live up the hollow a piece from where Jesse Stuart lives. Bud Adams farms the W-Hollow land on shares. The Adams family—Bud and his wife and their son (who was off somewhere the day I visited)—are Kentucky hollow prototypes: beautiful people. Bud Adams has the lean and hungry look of a wary mountain man, but if you're introduced properly, the wariness goes skittering. Suspicion is what we outlanders have colored these eastern Kentucky men with. It really isn't there at all. They're a kind and gentle people, hard because eastern Kentucky isn't the easiest land; generous, but I sense they could turn mean if crossed. They are a wiry and a muscular people. No city fat drags them down.

Bud Adams and his fine wife have many duplicates in the Appalachian mountains. You see them tending gas pumps in front of rickety stores on little-used county roads. You see them coming out of mines, out of fields, out of factories, out of beer halls, and out of mountain hollows that are misty— and they all seem exactly the same: purposeful people who can chop wood, hunt squirrels, plow the side of a mountain, build a cabin, and boil potatoes. The world beyond the hollows—in Ashland, say, or Cincinnati—has gone whistling by them, leaving them on the front porches of the past, swapping stories and wondering with mountain loneliness when they will come to Easy Street. I have seen these self-sufficient people transplanted to city slums, leaning out tenement windows, the last of their tribe, watching a city they don't understand. Now television antennas bristle from the roofs of their cabins, cottages, and shacks in the hollow. Artificial siding sometimes covers the original log walls of their tumbledown ancestral homes. Junk cars sometimes sit out front, rusting away.

They are a proud people for the most part. They are the sort you'd want to be stranded on a desert island with. With them, you could survive. They'd like desert islands. No tobacco base. They could grow as much as they pleased.

Give these people honest return for honest effort and you can trust them with your life. Jesse Stuart has faith in these eastern Kentucky people. I have, too, and my faith was reinforced, talking with Bud Adams. If there were a million of them spotted here and there in industry and on the college campuses, the beauty and worth of them would improve the rest of the breed.

We sat talking: me, Bud Adams, and his wife. The television was on. We talked, but kept one ear cocked for the noon news. The day before, tragedy had come to Greenup County. Mrs. Adams wanted to hear the details of it, to see if, perhaps, any kin were involved. The bodies of three men and three women from their county had been found in a hollow, victims of a one-car accident that had happened over the weekend. Their death car, as the Ashland paper described it, had been found lying on its side at the bottom of a cliff. Nobody knew whether the car's occupants had died slow or fast, and the hollow wasn't telling. To live in Greenup County is to live rubbing elbows with wilderness as well as rubbing elbows at the shopping center.

Mr. Adams looked at me thoughtfully. I had asked him about his poet-employer.

"Well," said Mr. Adams, "he's kind of hard to put in words. He's a splendid man. He's this type: if he thinks anyone is in distress, he'll go to 'em. The people that lived around here couldn't pay their rent one year and the owners had set them out. Well, this old lady was around eighty years old and there she sat, in the middle of all her belongings, a-crying, beside the road. Mr. Stuart had her stuff loaded up and brought up here and gave her a home. Went to work and got her an old-age pension check and everything. He does lots of stuff like that, Mr. Perry. He's that type."

His wife nodded.

On the television somebody was selling us a bra.

"I just don't know how to explain his goodness either," Mrs. Adams said.

"He thinks the world of you two," I said. Jesse Stuart had bragged on them a lot. "He said most tenant farmers wouldn't put as much effort into the land as the two of you do."

Mr. Adams nodded once, accepting this. I could sense his pride rising and it had reason.

"Well," he said, trying to avoid sounding "braggy," "we put as much into her as we can. If I don't make him no money, I can't make any money for myself. You got to take an interest in anything if you want to make money at it, don't you? Jesse's given us an awful good show here. He's been good to us, him and Deane both. They've been as good to us as they can be."

On the television somebody was selling us hair spray.

"He's a wonderful person," said Mrs. Adams. "He's the kind of person that has got a lot of nervous energy. He's got a sister exactly like him. All his sisters live around here. But one sister is nervous like he is. She's just a go-getter. And Jesse can't be still. You probably know that by talking with him. He can't sit down and talk to you. He's rubbing his face. He's rubbing his hands. He's crossing his arms." She crossed hers when she said this, as if it were catching. "But I guess that's the way they are. For a while, before I got acquainted with his sister, I thought maybe his heart attack had been caused by his nervousness. But evidently since his sister is so much like him, it just must be their way of doing."

She glanced at the television. The noon news was starting. The newscaster was telling of Vietnam. She turned back to me, but listened with one ear cocked for the local news.

"Has Jesse Stuart changed much in your opinion since his heart attack?" I said.

She made a motion with her hands.

"Well, now," she said, "I wasn't personally acquainted with him before the heart attack. I knew his mother real well. She was in the church we all went to. And I knowed her, but as far as Jesse goes, I didn't know him too well. I knew his writing, though. The neighbors around here are always talking about it. So when our son started to high school, he checked out some of Jesse's books and though he changed the names, I knowed everybody he was writing about, and their stories, even before he finished them."

"Did he tell of the people correctly?" I said.

"Every word he puts down," she said, "rings true. I've heard others tell about Jesse and they all say the same. They tell about how he would sit behind the old cookstove on the cookstove box and study sometimes till four o'clock in the morning. He was just a bookworm and he was one of the smartest boys you ever saw. He went barefoot and wore his britches with one leg hitched up and the other down. . . ."

The man on the television was showing us pictures of President Nixon talking somewhere.

"A lot of people come to the hollow to see Jesse Stuart, the author," I said. "Do they ever come back here in the hollow beyond his house down there?"

"Land," said the lady, "they *all* stop here and ask about him, you know, and that kind of stuff."

"If he ever done anybody wrong," said Mr. Adams gently, "I wouldn't know who it would be. And oh, the good he has done. He's just wonderful."

He thought upon this, then added:

"Why, he's the type of guy that goes out—all out—to help people get jobs. They go to him and he just does it. He knows practically everybody. You'd be surprised the people he's helped get jobs. He's been good to our son. We only have the one and Jesse just goes to bat for him and helps him in every way."

"He was telling me," I said, "about some high school boys he was working. He says he never really goes out to check on how they're doing. But he knows his land well enough to know whether they've done the job or not."

Mr. Adams agreed.

"He never checks on nobody," the tenant farmer said. "If he has them working and they go down and tell him how much time, he'll sit down and write them a check. He trusts us. Well, I'd trust him with my life. And I guess he'd trust us with his. We won't try to take nothing off him or nothing like that. The cabin up there on the ridge and all, everything is partners, half-and-half."

His wife nodded. That is the way things are, her nod said.

"How many hours a day do you work?" I said. "How many days a week?"

Mrs. Adams jumped into the conversation quickly. "He works," she said. "He works hard."

"Well," said Mr. Adams, honest as the day is long, "I don't put in too many. I generally try to work eight hours," he added.

"Today," said Mrs. Adams, "is his sixtieth birthday."

Pride radiated between the two of them. It seemed to fill the clean and neat room with sunshine as bright as the sunshine outside.

The man on the television was selling us instant coffee.

"I used to work a full day," Mr. Adams said, "dawn to dark. But I can't stand that much any more. I've done a lot of hard work in my life. Jesse's got a farm down there on the river. I take care of it, too."

"Does the farm down there flood out much?" I said.

That's what the river does to bottom lands. The snow melts in the mountains and all the water comes moving down the river sometime in early spring, bringing with it the rich topsoil and the chicken houses and the dead twigs it found upstream. Some spring floods are piddling and dinky affairs, hardly more than someone upstream spitting, but others, like the one in 1937, are powerful and muddy and dangerous, inundating entire river communities. People who farm the river bottoms look upon the spring floods as mixed blessings. If the flood comes, so does good soil. Or sometimes the river will get cantankerous and take the good soil away, leaving nothing but silt and junk earth on which only weeds can take root.

"Yep," said Mr. Adams. "She floods down there. The river backs in and makes the soil good."

"Then you're not exactly *on* the river?" I said.

"We're on her," he said. "The worst time is during the spring of the year down there. When the river comes up in, it takes forever for it to get out of there. Trying to get a crop out is trouble. Most of the low ground there is in grass. We don't farm that. We've had it in feed and grain the last four, five years," he added.

"How big is the river farm?"

He rubbed his jaw, calculating.

"Fifty-five acres, I would say," he said.

"All tillable?" I said.

"Yeah," he said. "Every foot of it, all excepting maybe just a little draining."

"And up here in the hollow," I said, "how much land do you actually work out of the thousand acres?"

He puzzled on that before answering.

"Well," he said finally, "taking in all these hills that's cleaned up around here, there must be three hundred acres working. Hay and tobacco is about all we farm now. And there's pasture."

"What's the tobacco base?" I said.

"An acre and four-tenths," he said.

"And how much hay would you have over the years?"

He shrugged.

"Up here on the farm," he said, "there's not too much where they can hay."

He pondered a little longer.

"I would say," he said, "around one hundred acres up here. On this farm. Not counting the one by the river."

"And the rest is timber and pasture?" I said.

His wife nodded. "You see," she said, "Jesse has got a lot of virgin timber in here. A lot of this place is woods and virgin timber."

The man on the television was telling us about the Cincinnati Reds.

"We keep our pastures mowed and trimmed just like a yard," Mr. Adams said. "What we can't get with a tractor, we go in and do her by hand."

To turn a mountain forest into a parkland did not seem to Mr. Adams to be farfetched. He was of the land and loved it, too.

"Do people come in here and picnic much?" I said.

"Not often," said Mrs. Adams.

"They'd leave the gates open and let the cattle out," complained Mr. Adams.

"How many cattle does Jesse Stuart have now?" I said.

"About sixty head right now," calculated Mr. Adams. "It runs anywhere between fifty and seventy."

"Do you ever use any of the timber?" I said.

That seemed to shock him.

"No," he said, looking pained. "Won't cut *any* of it."

His wife agreed.

"When Jesse builds a fence or anything," she said, "he generally buys posts rather than cutting them. Once in a while, some will be cut, but not often. They'll get a load or two of logs where they've blowed down. They'll blow down and he'll go out and cut logs off of that. They'll take it and have it sawed in lumber, but unless a tree *dies* or something like that..."

She smiled at me, hoping I would understand. She seemed pleased that I did. She had in her the same feeling her husband and Jesse Stuart had in them: a vague troubling where city people are concerned. City people—in this land of virgin timber and park-like wildernesses—were the destroyers who left gates unfastened so cattle could get out, who let burning cigarettes fall and create great fires, who left beer cans strewn along the road, who would chop down trees without a sense of loss in order to get quick profit. The city people: destroyers. It showed in the eyes of the Adams family and I had sensed it in Jesse Stuart's eyes, too. Their eyes seemed to mourn now and then with this sad knowledge.

"How many miles of rail fence would you say there is around here?" I said.

"We got board fence up this way," Mrs. Adams pointed out. "The rail fence is where they lay up and across like that."

"A rail fence is split out," said Mr. Adams, with the same kindness. They were both involved in my instruction. "They go out in the woods and cut the tree down and split by hand, but the board fence like this far up the hollow is nailed up."

"That rail fence down near the house where Jesse lives," said Mrs. Adams, "was built long before we came here. I don't know exactly how old it is."

"This up here ain't that old," he said.

"The barn up here looks older than the house," I said. "Which came first?"

"We built this house," said Mrs. Adams.

"There was a house here," said Mr. Adams. "But it was an old one. When we moved up here you couldn't get any farther than the foot of the hill down there."

"Do you get snowbound in winter?" I said.

"They have a boy on the tractor come by," Mrs. Adams said. She turned back to the matter of the house. You could feel her pride in it. She had reason to have pride. "We lived for years down there on Route Seven," she said. "I didn't like it down there. The water was so bad. The ground was no good. I let my husband talk me into staying there for five years, though. But Jesse said, after we had lived there the first year, that he would keep the house we were in as long as we wanted to stay there. 'When you leave,' he said, 'I'm selling.' Well, I was praying we'd come up here into the hollow. One day my husband came down here to the creek to get the tractor and I was sitting in the truck, waiting. Another guy came up to me to ask if I knowed where my husband was at. Pretty soon, Jesse came along and we all got to talking and Jesse said to me, 'Are you going to stay down where you're at?' and I said, 'I don't like it there and I'm not staying' and he said, 'Well, all right, why don't you come up here? Which house do you want?' I said the one that was here before and he said, 'You get anything you want to fix that little house up and I'll see that you get as good a house as the house I got.' He said, 'It's good news that you're coming because I need somebody here like your husband I can depend on.' He said, 'The cattle is there, I'll put the feed in the barn, you feed 'em and take care of them.' So he went back to the house and we went to work in the tobacco—and here we are. That other house, the one that was here, was little and so dirty. The paper on the wall was black. You couldn't tell what color it had been before at all."

She would have gone on, but the announcer was telling us of the six dead in Greenup County. Mr. and Mrs. Adams listened, leaning forward to stare at the announcer's eyes, testing the truth of him.

Then, the news done, Mrs. Adams turned the television off. She made a helpless motion.

"Awful," she said. "That was awful. Those poor, poor people."

"It happened just off Highway Seven," Mr. Adams said. He was sad, too.

"You come up and the road turns off and comes around...." said Mrs. Adams, reconstructing the death scene. "My, they say they plunged over two hundred feet."

Silence.

Then, I said, "Was the first house right here, too?"

They shook off the sadness. I was company.

"Yes," said Mr. Adams. "The little house was right where this one sets. We tore it down."

"If I were you," I said, "I'd want to stay here forever."

He agreed.

"I guess we'll die here," he said, a realist. "I tried to buy a little place he had over in Ohio but he wouldn't sell it to me. Well, he didn't want us to move. That was the main thing. And I told him, 'Jesse, I'll never leave as long as I'm able to work. When I get too disabled to work, then I'll move out of here and give it to somebody.' He said it was up to me, that here was my home. So I figure I'll leave well enough alone."

The country transaction impressed me. "If," I said, "this were in the city, you'd each write down a thousand different clauses in some kind of contract. But here, you just shake hands on it, and it's just as binding."

Mr. Adams nodded approval.

"Well," he said, "Jesse don't mess with me and how I do. He don't run around telling me what to do. He don't come up and say do it this way or do it that way. He just turned it over to us and that was that."

I felt a surge of pleasure. Here was pride—true pride —that was fresh as the hollow breeze. I had seen the counterparts of Mr. Adams—sixty-year-old men from the hollows as they padded, humped, along slum streets of a slum neighborhood they didn't understand. I had seen the pain in their eyes, emptiness and surrender. "Strangers and afraid, in a world they never made"—that's how another poet had summed up some human beings. I was pleased at the complicated interworkings of the world: somewhere in some bookstore someone had purchased a book that Jesse Stuart had written; the monies the writer derived from that one sale had bought nails that Mr. Adams used to nail a W-Hollow fence. From the book the unknown reader had achieved, while he was reading, a brief escape into the hills and hollows where another man, because of the book, could exist with pride. Yet, I had the feeling that had the unknown buyer of the book met Mr. Adams, say, on the streets of Ashland, each would have passed the other with hardly a glance, feeling they had nothing at all in common.

"It's really *your* place in a way," I was saying.

Mr. Adams agreed.

"If I need a piece for a tractor," he said, "if I break down or if the farm needs something, I go out and buy it. I get the bill. Jesse mails them a check for their money. I don't have to

go running around hunting him whenever I need something
here."

Or *beg* him or *justify* the need. This was unsaid but *there*.

"He travels a lot," I said. "I suppose there are times he
would be hard to track down."

I grinned. For a moment I had the fleeting and impossible
picture of Jesse Stuart, astride a camel, peering with wonder
at a pyramid when in the distance, driving a farm tractor
through the desert, comes Mr. Adams with a shopping list
needing filling: salt for the cattle, some fence posts, rigging,
this and that. No, Jesse Stuart traveled too much. He had
need of a man like Mr. Adams, a take-charge man of the hills.

"It's not too many times they're gone that we don't know
where they're at or where we can find 'em," said Mrs.
Adams.

Mr. Adams agreed.

"They never go off without telling," he said, with country
simplicity.

"She gives us the key to their house, if they're gone," said
Mrs. Adams, implying the trust. "If I need in the house for
anything, I can go anytime."

"But when they go off," I said, "for weeks or months at a
time, it seems like it would be easy for someone to come into
the hollow and get in their house. You're too far back in the
hollow to keep watch, aren't you?"

Mr. Adams shrugged.

"Well," he said, "that house won't be setting down there
by itself. We stay down there."

The glint in his eye was assurance enough.

"It wouldn't do," Mrs. Adams was saying, "to leave that
house just set there."

"They ain't about to break in when Jesse and Deane are gone," said Mr. Adams. "If somebody breaks into there, they're liable to be packed out."

Isolation was the key to W-Hollow. Isolation is a two-way street. It is both sanctuary and danger.

Mrs. Adams recollected that "somebody broke into his niece's house last Friday, right in the broad daylight. One time, just after we moved here and Jesse was gone, Deane was coming home from Greenup. It was in the afternoon. She came back and she said as she went in the front door, she heard somebody go out the back."

That bothered me.

"Wasn't that frightening?" I said. "She was there by herself. But everybody around here seems to carry a gun," I added.

Mr. Adams corrected me fast.

"Well, *I* don't," he said. "All I know is, down there they got a lot of old antique stuff in that house. Some people would love to get in there to get that. As for me, the only thing I could do with any of it would be to sell it. I'm not good at antiques. I wouldn't take care of it none, hardly at all. But Jesse and Deane are the kind that appreciates that stuff. That stuff is important to them, all of it."

We sat in silence. We had pretty much talked ourselves out. So I stood and said, "I want to thank you for letting me barge in like this and—"

They walked me to the door, giving me no time for my own amenities because they had theirs to express.

"You're more than welcome, Mr. Perry," Mr. Adams said. "The plain fact is, Jesse is such a good person you hardly know how to come to *explain* it to a man."

We stood on the porch in the sun of noon. Below us, the hollow road that led through the narrow hollow back to where Jesse Stuart lived. Above us, higher ground and cattle and stands of trees and sky. The only sound was the wind through the leaves of the trees. Other than that: hill-and-hollow silence.

"He used practically the same words about you," I told Mr. Adams.

But I had the lonely feeling time was playing tricks on me. Was this Mr. Adams—or the duplicate of Jesse Stuart's own father? This was the way I pictured Jesse Stuart's father to be: old and sinewy and wise and of the land, wise without the words to express the wisdoms, possessed by a feeling for the soil and fencerows and the timber. What Jesse Stuart had written of his father could easily apply to Mr. Adams, who stood beside me then, squinting at me in the brightness of the sun.

The poet had written:

> *And is he of the hills? He's of their dirt*
> *And all this hill-man knows is work and work.*
> *The color of the sun is in his face,*
> *The pick and adz have calloused his bare hands,*
> *The weights of loads he lifts have curved his back.*
> *But by hardships of life he understands*
> *How fine it is to own his humble shack,*
> *His fifty acres and his mules and plows—*
> *"This place to live, a place to die."*
> *Depository for him in the end,*
> *The earth at last becomes his bosom friend,*
> *He's of the dirt and he'll go back to dirt.*

His life will ripen like weeds on the hill
When they are sickled by untimely frost,
And when his work is done he will lie still,
Though his dust to the earth will not be lost . . .

Which was the father? And which the tenant farmer?
Were they truly both of the same cloth and somehow truly
one? Did Mr. Adams, as Jesse Stuart's father had done, "go
among his corn at night after his day was done—by lantern
light?"Was the love of Mr. Adams the love of Jesse Stuart's
father: " 'autumn when dead leaves rain and cornfields whis-
per?' " Mr. Adams, I was certain, could do as Jesse Stuart's father had done: "Use a cutter plow and axe, a mattock, spade,
pitch-fork and scythe and hoe . . ." I tried to make the mood
go away, but it lingered, all the pieces and words of it, and
there was Mr. Adams squinting at me in the sun and there
was his fine wife beside him.

Mr. Adams was squinting at me in a friendly manner and
saying:

"It's not just Jesse that's good, it's both of them. They're
both so good you don't know how to commence explaining
them to others."

He looked about him: surveying the land. He spoke again,
his voice eastern Kentucky–gentle.

"Before I came here," he said, "Jesse couldn't seem to get
nothing done around here. Now, Jesse is the kind that likes
to keep his ground neat, around the house and all around the
place. He wants everything kept neat. No papers blowing
around, nothing like that. He wants to keep her all looking
good. Well, I try my best to do it. Many is the time me and
my wife go up and down W-Hollow Road right down there

where sometimes spooners park of a night. We pick up the beer cans they throw away. Me and her will take the truck and go up and down there, going over it good, picking up old beer cans and old beer bottles and things, and we'll haul 'em off and throw them in the junk pile."

Mrs. Adams nodded agreement.

I was glad I had met them both. "You don't do those things because you *have* to," I said, "but because you *want* to—and I think that's pretty wonderful. You and the Stuarts are friends. It shows. It really does."

Mr. Adams digested this a moment. Then he said, "Yes, we don't *have* to do those things, but we do them in order to *please* Jesse and Deane. Since he likes things clean, I'll go ahead and do all I can to please him by keeping the place nice-looking for him. I like to keep him happy. He's easier to keep happy than most I've seen. He never knows when I'm going to mow or do this or that. He just comes by now and then and looks her over and sees that it is done. He's no boss. He's a friend. And he can't be explained. I can't commence to explain the goodness of him and his wife. . . ."

You might look upon Mr. Adams and his wife—and their affection for the Jesse Stuarts—as affected, corny, and foolish in this day and age when all the valentines seem angry. But Mr. Adams and his wife are real—and angry valentines are not.

NINE

OUT back of Jesse Stuart's home, up the hill a ways, is a bunkbuilding that contains thousands and thousands of magazines. Jesse Stuart is a "magazine" man. He wrote for them—still does—but the magazines these days are fewer. He and I stood in the bunkhouse, which contained, other than the many magazines neatly stacked, a few old and weathered traveling trunks that had been around the world and looked it. One Jesse Stuart had purchased in 1937 in Italy—leather was cheap there then, since Italy had a finger in Africa and grabbed up hides for a song. But the magazines impressed me most: thousands of them.

"These are collectors' items," I said, "even if some don't have your articles in them."

"My goodness, yes," the poet said. "But magazines are dying. A couple of good magazines have kept up, but most haven't. The *quality* doesn't seem to be there any more, Dick. Some of the little magazines are dandies, though. What did you think of that one I showed you from Ohio State University? But I'll bet that magazine doesn't have over a thousand subscribers. I've not subscribed to it, but I'm going to. I really shouldn't. I don't have time to read all my mail now. Naomi Deane and I are readers, but where's the time to read?

We've taken as many as forty different magazines at a time and have no time to read them."

And *saved* every one of them, I wanted to say, looking at the shelves and shelves of them, but I said nothing. We each put things aside we intend *someday* to read, but *someday* never rolls around.

"Oh," Jesse Stuart was saying, "we glance through them when they arrive and maybe read a little of them, but not much. I like the foreign magazines, too. The British ones are excellent. I used to take a magazine from Pakistan. It was published in English. And after I'd been to the Philippines, I took one of their magazines, too. Got to knowing it and got to liking it, but eventually I let the subscription run out. There wasn't time to read it. The printing of it wasn't the best, but the contents were excellent. It was a combination of the old *Saturday Evening Post* and the *Literary Digest*. They say Roosevelt's election killed the *Literary Digest*. They had predicted that he would be defeated and he wasn't. That pulled the rug out from under them and the magazine just died. . . ."

Others have died or dwindled into something else. Once-great literary magazines no longer appeal to the literary. The magazines these days, Jesse Stuart and I felt, are little more than duplicates of television, printed on paper and sent through the mail instead of through the airwaves. Quarterlies abound, of course, but they do not have the mass appeal that great literary magazines once had. Each quarterly, we decided, appeals to an ever-decreasing circle, whose interests become more and more specific. The magazine racks today have much reading material, but the literary adventure has gone skittering.

Gone is *Liberty*, gone is *Collier's*, gone is the *Saturday Evening Post*. Where did *St. Nicholas* magazine vanish to? And *Scribner's Magazine?* They have been largely replaced on the magazine racks by how-to-do-it hot-rod magazines and magazines filled with sensual but untrue confessions.

"I made *Scribner's*," said Jesse Stuart. There was pride in his voice. I envied him that accomplishment. "I sold them poetry and short stories. I made *Atlantic* and *Harper's* and *Esquire* and Mencken's old greenback, *Mercury*. That was one of the best magazines this country ever had, Dick. I even made the *North American Review* that first published *Thanatopsis*. There was another good magazine. It ran for about a century before it died, but time caught up with it, too, and there she went. I get some awful good feelings about some of those magazines. I've always loved good magazines. I have the strange feeling that pretty soon *all* the magazines will be gone. Most have left already, haven't they? If it weren't for the regional presses and the university magazines, I don't know what would happen to our magazine world. But even those magazines can't survive by themselves. They have to be supported by universities."

"And their circulation is limited," I said.

He agreed.

"There must be some way those circulations could be built up," he said, but sensed the helplessness of the idea. To be a writer these days is to be a realist. "If they got some good promoters, they could build up into pretty good magazines, couldn't they? And if they would *pay* authors something, I think that would be marvelous. Some of them do pay as much as fifty dollars a story, but that's not really enough. They can't afford to pay more, though. I've just had an acceptance from the *Southwestern Review,* one of the best magazines in the United States today—and they pay a little. Not much. I've known the editor there about thirty years."

We stepped outside the bunkhouse into the sunshine. We stood and talked about the dollar side of this writing profession. Truth is, there are few full-time free-lance writers and poets. Most need other jobs—in universities, advertising agencies, newspapers, farming, bricklaying, or bartending—to support the muse. The free-lance writer who tells you he's free-lance usually isn't; he's only partially free-lance. Most of us, Jesse Stuart and I decided, who live by the typewriting drippings live a free but hand-to-mouth existence. Those are the facts of our lives.

"The average person writing," I said, "would have a hard time knowing all the obscure little quarterlies."

Jesse Stuart agreed.

"That's why I tell new writers to buy that book called *Writer's Market,*" he said. "It has the little markets listed."

"But no more can a fellow try his hand at turning out a 'short-short' story for *Liberty,*" I said.

This saddened us. What writer of our vintage hadn't tried to turn out a quickie for *Liberty?* The memory made us brothers who suffered the same pain.

"*I* tried to write 'em for *Liberty,*" said the poet. "I tried hard. But I could never sell them."

"Me, neither," I said. "They always had a twist at the end of each story, like 'and the man was blind.' "

Jesse Stuart brightened.

"Wouldn't O. Henry have fared well with them!" he said. "But he missed them. He was before their time, I guess."

"Many writers who started that way couldn't start today at all," I said. "The magazines are gone. There would be nowhere the writer could be published."

We began to stroll down the steep hillside to the house. Jesse Stuart was saying, "I can recall some of them who were in those magazines. One of them was William Saroyan. Harry Sylvester was another. You probably never heard of him. He did an awful lot of sports things for *Collier's*. He wrote steady for them. He was a Notre Dame football player before he started writing. My goodness, I believe *Scribner's* published some of his stories, too. There were just any number of good magazines for men back in those days. That was the trend back then."

We paused to watch a redbird fuss with another redbird in the dogwood tree. Then one bird flew away, angry, and that was that. We continued to stroll back to the house.

"Consider Whit Burnett," said Jesse Stuart. "Look what he could do with a story. He and Martha Foley started *Story Magazine*. When you got a story by him and into his magazine, you were really something; you had *made* it! He's the one who used to edit *This Is My Best*. He took my *first* story," he added, with awe that lingered over the years.

We went into the house and settled in one of the living rooms.

"When you got into *Story Magazine*," he reaffirmed, "all the publishing houses began looking at you as a possible novelist or a non-fiction writer or biographer or dramatist or poet. Those were the shiny days of writing, Dick. Each editor wants to claim the honor of producing and publishing as many new writers today as Whit Burnett did back then, but none can hold a candle to him. Most of your best writers back then were discovered first by Whit Burnett and his magazine. I think we all ought to get together and give him some kind of a pension. He's done so much for literature, he shouldn't have to work any more. He's done a lot for me. He's done a lot for William Saroyan. He almost got Faulkner and Thomas Wolfe. He had them early in their careers. I can safely say that Whit Burnett started at least fifty of the country's best writers. Without him, the writers might not have made it at all."

A pleasant thought that somewhere in the literary innards of commercial publishing a guardian angel existed. But that was in the past; I was concerned about today. What of the new writers coming on? Who would comfort them? I had to ask the question:

"That's fine, Jesse, but who is doing that today for writers?"

The poet shrugged.

"Whit Burnett is back at it," he said. "But there's nobody else that I know of other than him. I don't know of a single soul that's doing it. Oh, there might be somebody but he can never do it the way that Whit Burnett did. You might be interested in his background. He was from Utah. He was born a Mormon. Only he got away from there and came east. You should have seen him, Dick. He looked like Chaucer. He was about the size of Chaucer and he had a beard like Chaucer and he was built like the pictures I've seen of Chaucer. I always liked Whit Burnett. When I first got to New York he was one of the first that I looked up. But do you know something? He never had much money. He never made much, either. I wonder sometimes how he actually survived, but boy, he's done something for America. He wrote just one book about the struggles he was having. He was a fine man and a fine editor. He called his book *The Literary Life and the Hell with It.*"

Money—and the muse. Where writers are concerned, the two are practically strangers.

But if the world of short-story writing had diminished, there was another writing world that had never truly blossomed—financially, that is—at all.

"You never made much money as a poet, did you?" I said.

"A few dollars," Jesse Stuart said. "And that's about the size of it."

"Which means," I said, "there can never be a full-time poet, living off his poetry."

"You're absolutely correct. On two occasions I've sold poems for five hundred dollars but those occasions were rare."

"In other words," I said, "as a poet you write your soul out and starve."

"That's the way *all* writing is," he said. "You don't get much for any of it. How much do you make from your books? You could make more laboring, couldn't you? So could I. I feel sorry for all of us that have to write. We give all we've got, we can't get free of writing, and we're stuck. It's a hard way to make a living and most of the time a thankless way. Look at the poets. As I said, I got five hundred dollars for two poems—and that was the exception. Two magazines bought 'em, but that was back then. Today they wouldn't touch 'em."

"Yet," I said, "had you written an article or a story, you would have made two or three thousand dollars from the sale, wouldn't you?"

He nodded. "That's right."

"But doesn't the same amount of energy go into a poem?" I said.

"More goes into a poem," he answered fast, rubbing his crew cut. "More goes into 'em. One of those poems I sold was *Love Song after Forty*. The magazine that bought it kind of broke it up. I had sent them two copies and they said it was a poem but they wanted to publish it in prose form because prose form occupied less space and they could get more ads in the magazine. So I said, 'Go ahead and do what you want.' The same poem was titled *Kentucky Is My Land*; they published it in Louisville and it's now a collector's item. Everybody is crying to have a copy; so Ashland Oil and Refining Company up here is putting it out again. Bankers have used it. I don't know who all have used it. They had asked me to describe the state. The magazine had said to me, 'Now you can write poetic prose, so we want to know a little about the blue grass, the horse racing—all of your state.' Well, that poem covered the state. And it was used in a Scott-Foresman textbook that went around the world. All I ever made from it was five hundred dollars."

That aroused my curiosity.

"How much would you say you've made from your poetry," I said, "since you first began writing it?"

He shrugged.

"Dick," he said, "I'd be ashamed to tell you. Now, let's see." He began reckoning in his head. "One of the books that's paid me the best—and this will surprise you—was the last one from McGraw-Hill. It's called *Hold April*. I think the book sells for four ninety-five. I get ten percent a book, or about a half dollar. So I'll probably make nearly five thousand dollars from it. That seems a lot, but consider how many poems I've written and published for nickels and dimes: close to two thousand poems! *Esquire* has paid me for some poems. Actually, *Esquire* has been one of the best to me with poetry and they don't usually publish poetry! They published this one poem of mine that I wrote on Lyndon Johnson. I got three hundred dollars for it. That's the satire that starts out, 'How like the great Greek God Apollo is our king. . . .' And they paid me three hundred dollars for the John L. Lewis poems that were satire, too. Then they've paid me one hundred dollars a time or two. I suppose I've made close to a thousand dollars on poems from *Esquire* magazine. And when do you ever *see* poems in that magazine? So *Esquire* has helped me. And *Hold April* has helped me. But this is unusual, in a way. Ask any publisher. Some publishers won't touch a book of poems by me. I just couldn't get the publisher to reissue *Kentucky Is My Land* even though there was a demand for it. Being a poet is not easy."

"Did you publish it yourself then?" I asked.

"Yes," he said. "But I made practically nothing on it. Now, you take *Man with a Bull-tongue Plow*. It sold a little, not much. Yet, everybody thinks I made a fortune on that book. And there's *Album of Destiny*. Some out there say it's the greatest book I've ever written, but it never sold well. It just never caught on. A man came here the other day, a connoisseur of good books, and he said if he was to take one book to an island with him, he would take *Album of Destiny*. I worked eleven years on that book, Dick! Look at the time: eleven years! And all I probably made off it was five hundred dollars. That's all. Now, it's a collector's item.

"Dutton only sold twelve hundred copies of *Kentucky Is My Land.* I had it reprinted and sold six thousand and then some."

"But," I said, "you could have lost your shirt by publishing it privately."

He agreed.

"Sure, I could have," he said. "I sure could have lost my shirt. But you see doing it privately, I got a better percentage of the cover price. *I* was the manufacturer as well as the author. But I put it out on a good basis. I never sent it anywhere out of Kentucky, except to Georgia Glynn when she was running a department store book department in Cincinnati. She felt it would sell in Cincinnati. I said the title probably wouldn't appeal to Ohioans, but she said they had an awful lot of Kentuckians in Cincinnati, and she knew her business. They sold around five hundred books up there. Cincinnati was the only place out of the state I sold it, with the exception of Huntington up the river. The Kentucky Library Association took it, Kentucky parks sold it, and one woman in Louisville bought four hundred copies herself! Now it's out of print; there are no copies of it left. I made around five thousand dollars on that book published that way, privately. That's not bad pickings for a poet. But that's the only time I've ever done that and made a good profit and I'm not going to do it again. Putting out your own book is too much bother. But I declare, it was a beautiful job of printing, just beautiful. This Baptist minister up here did it for me. He prints beautifully. He's really a top printer, a fine man. So let's see, let's reckon some more. . . ."

He sat, muttering numbers at himself.

Then he said, "Let's say I've done pretty good with poetry. I believe I've brought in about fifteen thousand dollars
from my poetry altogether."

"But," I said, "could you have lived on that alone over the
years you were writing?"

He was quick to answer.

"My goodness, no," he said. "I'd have starved to death as
sure as I'm sitting here. Robert Frost never made it on poetry
alone and neither did Carl Sandburg. That's frightening when
you get right down to it," he added.

"When your poems are included in school textbooks," I
said, "if you get paid at all, do you get a flat fee?"

He nodded.

"That's right," he said. "A flat fee to the company and the
company divides it. I won't get much. Sometimes I'll get five
dollars and sometimes I'll get ten dollars. The fees are little,
very little. You get paid five dollars if they reprint your
poem." This made him sad. "You know, Dick, there's not a
poet on the face of the earth who would dissent with you
about poets not being paid enough. They will all agree that
poets simply can't live by poetry alone. It can't be done.
Truck drivers make big money. So do construction workers.
So do the men in the steel mills. So do head waiters. The emphasis in the United States is not on art. Why? Because who
goes out and buys art? They'll go out and buy what we don't
consider art at all. We consider it trash. And I could mention
a few to you, like these men who write these sexy detective
stories where women are getting shot in the stomach on
every page. Look at the millions of copies those books sell.
But do you ever see any parts of those reprinted in school
textbooks? No, sir! Of course you don't."

"Those are the books that seem to be written in three days," I said, "with a day-and-a-half break in the middle."

"But they make the money," said the poet. "Walt Whitman said it best one time. He said, 'To have great poets, we have to have great audiences.' Whitman said that himself. And look at him and how little he made. People that bought his books used to throw them at him. Yet, look where he fits today in literature."

"You could have doubled or tripled your income by playing to the gallery, couldn't you?" I said.

"If I had been a businessman, Dick," he said, "I actually believe that with a little luck, I could have ended up a millionaire. If I had been a businessman, I would have gone after it tooth and nail. If I had worked at business the way I have worked at writing, I could have been a millionaire easily."

Writers, it is said, exhaust themselves the way actors do: by the time the old theatrical ham heads over the hill to the poorhouse he has worn his emotions down to a frazzle because the portrayal of emotions is the only trick in his bag. Writers exhaust themselves verbally, reducing all humanity to the printed page, parsing every emotion to portray its component parts in paragraphs. By the time the old *writer* heads over the hill to the poorhouse, he has so clearly defined everything that he senses only the uselessness of words. Some writers and actors seem happy on the surface. Inside, each is perhaps churning with needs and dreams unrealized. One of these is true success. True success, by honest terms, does not exist at all. No one ever writes well enough. No one is ever paid well enough. No one is ever completely understood. The writer and the actor, both tuckered out, look at other fields, all of which look greener. Would Jesse Stuart have become a millionaire? I doubt it and so does he. Somewhere along the way, as Sherwood Anderson was, he would have been sidetracked by the muse.

"I'll tell you a secret," Jesse Stuart was saying, "that has never been printed. What I've done has not been guesswork. It has been planned, every last bit of it. Donald Davidson once told me there is so much material that has not been written about my Appalachian area that I had better get started writing it. He said, 'Jesse, go back to your land and write of your land and write of your people as William Butler Keats wrote of Ireland and as Robert Burns wrote of Scotland, and as Sir Walter Scott wrote of it, too. Go back, Jesse, and write of your people and of the things you know.' So that's what I've been doing ever since.

"Have you ever heard of a deep bench in football where they can pull reserves from? I've got a deep bench here in writing. I've got novels written that nobody has even seen yet, sitting back there on the shelves. For every thing I sent out to market, I wrote something else and set it aside. Some of the stuff needs changing, though, like the dialogue. The dialogue was written differently back in the thirties. People now wouldn't understand that dialogue. But it was correct for the period I wrote it. Some of the thoughts need changing, like what I thought of Herbert Hoover. Back in the early years of the depression we didn't think much of him and I'd want to cut stuff like that out because history has proved it wrong. Well, actually I burned the material about him. I didn't want it around."

Something troubled me. All writers have things tucked away: rough drafts of books, a few tries at a paragraph, a poem or so, perhaps a play. Most mean to tinker with the writing tucked away, but the time never seems to come. Pretty soon God whispers and the writer is gone, leaving behind writings he had wished to edit into shape. Someone else, without the writer's heart and point of view and skill, comes upon these writings and in a reckless moment tosses them off to publishers, who in an equally reckless moment palm the writings off on the public. The result: the writer is lessened by these unedited writings. His place in history goes down a notch or two. I talked about this with Jesse Stuart, in terms of the Hemingway material the public was now getting posthumously.

The poet had strong feelings on this.

"They never should have published most of it," Jesse Stuart said. "Look at what he wrote about Fitzgerald. Hemingway must have been jealous of him. Goodness, that Fitzgerald could write! Hemingway said some awful things about him."

I changed the subject.

"What made you keep going all these years?" I said.

"I had the drive to be a poet and to get an education," he said. "I've always had those two drives. A college degree was important to me. I was the first of my people to get one. I beat my cousin by two hours, or a day, or something like that. He was my former teacher. He was five years older than me but I beat him and was the first in the family to get a college degree."

"How are you with some of the fundamentalists, those academic people who might drain the creative juices out of you?"

"In a way," he said, "I guess you might say I am one of them. I'm a teacher. I have a degree and everything. And I

teach the way they do. Come to think of it, I *don't* teach the
way they do. I don't understand half of them and what they
are about."

"If they would write a review of your poetry, wouldn't
their academic interpretation frighten you?"

He perked up.

"Listen," Jesse Stuart said, "you saw that pile of scrapbooks I have, didn't you? They're filled with reviews I've
never read. I don't read reviews any more. All I do is paste
them in. Oh, my goodness, you'd be surprised at some of the
interpretations and some of the reviews I *have* read. Of
course, a writer likes to see if maybe the reviewer has caught
on to what the writer was writing about. Some of the reviewers and critics do, and when that happens any writer is
pleased. But on the other hand, you get these reviewers and
critics who don't know what the score is. For instance, I
brought out a novel *Daughter of the Legend* about a Melun-
geon girl. That's a race of people unknown to man; nobody
knows where they came from. It's the only race of people I
know of in the world that can't trace their origins. They're
down there in eastern Tennessee, but nobody knows where
they came from originally. They're a little bit in North Carolina and Virginia, too, as well as some—a few—in Kentucky. But not very many. I think there are only ten to
twenty thousand of them altogether. They're Americans.
Maybe Sir Walter Raliegh's Lost Colony and the Indians got
mixed up together somehow and produced them. They're
part Indian but they don't know what the other part of them
is: Portuguese or Spanish or what? So, anyway, I wrote this
story about this girl who was one of them. Somebody in
Louisville reviewed it for the newspaper. I think the reviewer

was a schoolteacher, teaching English in high school. She said that I had *created* a race of people out of my imagination and had built a novel about them so I could make money. Well, I tell you, the type wasn't cold in the newspaper before somebody got after her. He was a lawyer who had lived down among these people in the panhandle part of West Virginia. He told her off in no uncertain terms that these people had actually lived on his farm. Well, there you are. I'm just showing you how some reviewers and critics do their jobs. She didn't check to see if the people did exist. She had looked up the word in the dictionary and when she couldn't find it, she drew her own conclusions. That's how careless some reviewers are. Here was a girl, a college graduate, teaching high school English and *she* had *me* concocting a race. Can you imagine anything like that?"

"How did you respond to her?"

"Didn't," he said. "The lawyer did it for me better than I could have. Besides, I never respond. What's the use of it?"

Jesse Stuart was at peace and with good reason. Generally the critics had been kind to him, kinder than they are to most poets. And his fellow artists have been kind to him, too, for example, William Saroyan:

As I see it, Jesse Stuart is a natural. A natural is somebody who could be nobody very gracefully, but happens to have genius, and is therefore *somebody* very gracefully. He is anonymous and a personage at the same time. Any person capable of genius and anonymity simultaneously is a person who is truly great.... I think of him as an American Robert Burns. He is not a city-made writer, and in him is none of the irritation and confusion of the city-made writer. He is, and the people of his writing are, real, against a natural, not an artificial, background.... Stuart writes swiftly and abundantly, but he is not out of time with nature, so that among the younger writers of America, he stands out as one who is certain to stay, to work steadily, and to grow.

Saroyan's estimate of Stuart was given in *Jesse Stuart, His Life and Works*, a study by Everetta Love Blair, published by the University of South Carolina Press in 1967.

In the March–April 1940 issue of Dutton's *News of Books and Authors*, these paragraphs by Edgar Lee Masters appeared:

Jesse Stuart blew in on me last fall, and he was like a breeze from the hills. He is as full of life as a young colt, and as normal as earth.... I have such confidence in him that I would turn him loose in Boston for the rest of his life without any fear that Boston would ruin him. I'd say the same thing of New York. But if I know him, he will not leave his Kentucky hills. He is living in a day when there is no magic lure in the city. In Howells' time, Emerson and others were in or near Boston, and Howells went there. It is unfortunate when a young writer gets the idea that famous men have something to offer him beyond what they have put in their books. Howells got nothing except more book learning. He became an editor, and for one reason or another, grew more timorous and restrained. Jesse Stuart does not need to be told there is nothing in the Metaphysical poets of this day; he is not interested in theories, in gropings after the recondite, the vague thistle-wanderings of the imagination. By knowing life, and by devoted interest in it, he has all the criticism he needs.

I can't see anything that will turn him aside, blow him up, corrupt him. His feet are so firmly planted on nature that he is safe from all literary perils. His sense of humor is a help to salvation. He loves the hills there in Kentucky; he loves his mules; he loves to work with his hands, You can't beat such a man. He will write a good novel, and *Trees of Heaven* will be it. His short stories are fresh, original, and rich in human nature.

I had many fine talks with him last fall, full of fun, banter, story-telling, and comments on writers. I didn't offer him a word of criticism. He is a good tree and should be allowed to grow the way that nature wants him to. His own sap and roots will take care of the apples.

"Jesse," I said, "Walt Whitman wrote much in celebration of the people and the land. Do you feel sometimes like writing something which *doesn't* celebrate?"

The poet just smiled at me. He is a man who celebrates each dawn. But there are times when he feels the restless urge *not* to write. And being the writer that he is, he puts these moments into words. Across from me sat the poet who wrote:

> *I cannot write tonight for the moon is full*
> *And large as a wagon-wheel above the timber;*
> *I must go out for the world is beautiful,*
> *Must leave the open fire and dying ember.*

For what are words upon an ink-stained scroll
When magic moonlight floods this stubborn world,
When wary winds of ruthless winter roll
Over the knolls, and leaf and seed are hurled
Into illimitable starry space . . ."

TEN

JESSE STUART had the fidgets. He was nervous as a cat. For three days he had been trying to prod me out of their living room, into the car, to tour the 1000 diverse acres of W-Hollow. I had wanted to go, he had wanted me to go, but I had wanted to wait until I knew him better. To tour the hill-and-hollow land with someone you have just met is one thing. To tour it with someone you have studied carefully, and come to love, is much sweeter. *This* was why I had—impolitely, perhaps—put off the tour. I wanted to know the man before I knew his land. Does that make sense? To know the man, I sensed, would be to put the land into perspective. I was glad I waited. But, in the waiting, Jesse Stuart got the fidgets. He was a child with a new bicycle for Christmas, a bike the snow would not give him a chance to try.

As we settled in his little foreign station wagon in front of his house, I said:

"This should be a good little car for getting around your place in."

"Oh, she's a dandy," he said. "This little thing can go places the big one wouldn't dare to go."

We started up the hollow, away from the county road,

back to where the hollow began to close in on us tight, press-
ing at us with steep hills on either side. The hills seemed to go
straight up and down. The trees on them were bright with
the green of summer now. Jesse Stuart had once written of
them in the autumn.

> *I've seen the dead leaves start before my eyes*
> *And drift and drift into the windy skies.*
> *And I have heard the crisp air ring with cries*
> *Of birds now going to the south—I've heard*
> *The lost cries of these migratory birds*
> *Above the brown fields, beneath the windy skies—*
> *Sounds far too primitive for a poet's words . . .*

We were in September-land, driving up the ever-tighten-
ing hollow. Winter was around the corner, waiting with
chilly breath.

"This bottom along here," Jesse Stuart was saying, "we
made that. Not here, where she narrows, but yonder down
the road where the house is. The creek creeps like a snake
along here, winding in and out. Up there against the foot of
that hill I used to raise peanuts. I raised some good ones."

The road, now cramped in the hollow, was bordered by a
plank fence in good repair. Nearer the county road, behind
us, the fence was split-rail and dramatic. Along here, beyond
the eyes of travelers, the fence became modern and more
functional. The fence seemed to stretch before us forever, the
same as it stretched out in our wake.

"What season do you like best here?" I asked.

"April," he said without hesitation. "April, Dick, is out of
this world here. Just any normal April at that. I like October,
too. I—looky, see that hill right there." He pointed to the

hill that hemmed us in on the left. It seemed to rise up suddenly from the hollow and go slantways to the sky I could
not see. "When I was a little boy," Jesse Stuart said, "my dad
and me used to come here. There's a big beech there somewhere we'd tie the mule to. He used to farm the side of that
hill clear up to the top of her."

I was impressed. It was a sled-ride hill and steep. It seemed
to go straight up and down. A city farmer could never have
farmed that slope. He would have tipped over and fallen off.

"Yes, we farmed that," Jesse Stuart was saying. "The Sea-
tons owned this land then. There was no fence along here or
anything. We plowed that hill—that mountainside—
with a mule and plow, turning over the sod. My mother and
my dad hoed and plowed there many a spring and summer
day. I've farmed it myself many a time, too. There must be
sixteen good acres on that hillside. But steep land doesn't
measure like bottom land. It'll fool you every time."

We were farther up the hollow then, near the hollow's end.
The car maneuvered with bumps and wrenchings over the
road rocks and the rain ruts up a little grade. Jesse Stuart
passed the farm house where I had visited the Adams family.
Mrs. Adams, on the front porch, waved as we bounced by,
climbing higher up out of the hollow till we were in the high
world of pasture and forests. As he drove, Jesse Stuart kept
up a running commentary.

"Look at the white pines sticking up yonder," he said. "I'll
show you what we got up here. See that pasture beyond.
Look at the pines. Look at the forest. Do you know that we
farmed every bit of it when I was a young man? My mother
helped in there and so did my dad. We raised wheat in there
and we raised corn."

The car was perched on the edge of a pasture that was on

the edge of a hill. Where Jesse Stuart was pointing was another section of steep wilderness that seemed to me almost
straight up and down. He and his folks had farmed angry
land.

"But we farmed it anyway!" Jesse Stuart said when I told
him that. "We were a rugged people. Oh my goodness, just
think what we would have done on flat land like around Columbus, Ohio! That's something to ponder on, isn't it?"

It was.

We were, by then, bouncing through a forest on the top of
the hill. The ridgeline wasn't made with a ruler. Sometimes
we would dip into little pastures—a small boat at the bottom of a wave—and sometimes we'd be as high as man
could get, poised on the crest; then we would dip again into
more wilderness, dark with shadows where old trees kept the
sun away. All this was W-Hollow. But it was no forest tangle. All this was whistle-clean like a public park. The stands
of timber, which some view with dollar signs in their eyes,
Jesse Stuart viewed with love.

"See that little road going off over there?" he said, pointing
to a trace. "That's a fire road. We had some terrible fires
here. And looky over there. There's enough ash trees to build
yourself a fine home."

We arrived at a cattle fence. I got out, opened it, he drove
through, I closed it again, I got back in the car, and he started
up.

"You're not so 'city,'" he said. "I'm surprised. Thought
you would be city."

I had to dispel that illusion. "I'm city all right," I said. "But
I did used to write articles for *Farm Quarterly* magazine."

He nodded. "You got some country in you somewhere,"

he said. "You—" But the world distracted him. "Up here is
nice. There's no asthma up here on the ridge. I know my
brother-in-law got cured of it up here."

We moved out of the woods onto another pasture beyond
which seemed the sky.

"In a minute," he said, as the car bounced through the pasture, "I'll show you your native state, Ohio. I almost put a
house here in this pasture. Look at that electric line cutting
across. This was the only way they could run electricity back
to the hollow from Greenup. I let 'em do it. I was glad to.
They ran her right up the side of the hill from Greenup
down there."

We had reached where pasture met sky. Below us was the
Ohio River, Greenup, and the smudges of the industrial valley. I could see in the distance the gloom of the industrial sky
that morning over Ashland, and over Ironton on the Ohio
side of the river. But where we were, lone figures on the edge
of the palisade that dropped down into the smog of today,
there was fresh air. We were looking at a mural that moved,
lived, made smoke, and corrupted. But where we were was
sanctuary.

"Looky at the industry," said the poet. "There's Ohio.
There are *your* hills."

We did not linger. The view, impressive and a powerful
thing, seemed to make us both feel sad. W-Hollow, *his* land,
plunged over the side of that steep hill and went down into
that valley of the smog and noise: a memory butting heads
with a reality.

"I like your hills here," I said, to change the mood.

The poet in him responded.

"They come here," he said, "to get walnuts. See? This tree

has got a few left on it. There used to be plenty of chestnuts around here. There used to be persimmons and pawpaws." He glanced again at the valley. "This farm of mine goes down yonder nearly to Greenup," he said. The melancholy returned. "Some of these days, if the population comes the way they say, these hills of mine will be covered with homes. Nice ones, I hope. . . ."

Or little fenced-in lots, each the size of a postage stamp. Little box-like ticky-tacky houses, each the twin of the others, all with backyard grills and car porticos and wading pools and little twigs that developers call trees. We were, on the brow of that hill, like the Indians who must have watched with suspicion the log rafts of settlers drifting down the river west, hoping they would drift on by, never to put ashore, but knowing sooner or later they had to. There were so many of them and there were so few of us.

"Funny," Jesse Stuart was saying, trying to break the spell, "but we never farmed this cleared pasture up here. I don't know why. It wasn't always cleared, of course. We cleared it up and let it be. We farmed the hillside right down under us. I used to plow down there. We raised the best corn."

He drove away from the brim, back into the pasture, crossing it, and into another stand of trees. Cows grazed on the shadows. They did not mind us. They sought sustenance. The car was not their enemy. They sensed the car would never graze.

"Well, I declare," Jesse Stuart said, driving along. "Lightning has hit that tree. That must have happened since I was out here last."

He had memorized each and every tree that W-Hollow had.

"You'll like where I'm taking you now," he said. We

moved like thieves among the forest. "Trees are everywhere here, but in winter when the leaves are off, from this one spot you can see the Ohio River as well as the Sandy. The Sandy is broader here than the Ohio River is because it's been dammed by the new high-level dams they put in. Right here, in this woods, you're at the end. The ground slants down every way from here to the two bodies of water."

He pointed to another trace through the trees.

"I built this road," he said. "Cleared the timber and everything. This is a beautiful location, Dick, high up here, with the rivers down there. When the leaves are off, you would love it. From this spot you can get the best photographs of sunsets you'd ever want to get. When I bought this piece of land, nobody wanted it. They said I was foolish to buy it."

I looked down one slope.

"You did a lot of clearing here and down there, didn't you?"

He nodded.

"We used to farm that down there," he said of another slantways patch. "But now we must keep cattle up here, so we let it grow. Well, this is where this side of the farm ends, Dick. This used to be an old public highway along this ridge, until 1928. That's when they closed it up. This was where the first civilization, or the early civilization, was around here. There used to be a big hotel here amongst the trees on this ridge. There used to be a church. Why, I've found people who say they attended church up here."

Now, only the silence of the woods, only the ghostwhispers of the departed guests and worshipers.

"So you actually bought a township road?" I said, impressed. I was more "city" than I had thought.

"Yep," he said. "That's the old road. There she goes. They

built the roads on these ridges because here it was high and dry. People used to come up here a lot because those who lived in the valley had what they called the ague. They shook and got the shivers something awful, so they would come up here to get free of the chills and fevers the valley had."

"Do you ever ride through here?" I said. It was tremendous horse country.

"We used to," he said. "But not on riding horses. Farm horses . . ."

The car inched through the wet of the forest, following the road that only the Stuarts used. The road wasn't there. Only the cleared suggestion of it remained. Grass grew where the road had been, and so did milkweeds and little windflowers.

"In a novel of mine," Jesse Stuart said, "I wrote about this area up here. This is Laurel Ridge. An old character used to live up here, a squatter, before I bought the land. He was a prophet, he said. Well, when I bought the land I just let him stay. After all, he had squatted here long before I had anything to do with here."

We moved out of the forests into another clearing. In the pasture stood a red barn and a white frame cottage, both in good repair.

"He had himself a different cabin," Jesse Stuart said. "We fixed this one up ourselves, me and Naomi Deane. Here's where we come up and work sometimes to get away from it all. The cabin is here in the middle of nowhere. Nobody bothers it. It'll end up with electricity and be a fine little place. Naomi Deane is a really good housekeeper. She fixed it up beautifully."

We entered the little cottage. Its largest room was the

kitchen. Two little bedrooms were there. Light fixtures—
to which no electric lines were connected—were waiting.
Meanwhile kerosene lamps and lanterns were here and there.
The place inside was airy and light and clean, as if waiting
for the poet and his wife to visit again. Touches of home
were everywhere: pictures on the walls, shelves of condi-
ments, cooking utensils—and in one room: a desk and chair
awaiting the writer. I had the feeling it had been occupied
only moments before, and that its occupants were somewhere, strolling hand in hand, among the trees of the dark
forest.

"How far are we from your house in the hollow?" I said.

"A good two miles by car," he said. "If we walked up the
hollow from straight down there, it's only a mile, though."

"How long has the cabin been here?" I said.

"Since 1930, but we revamped it," he said. We stepped
outside again. Jesse Stuart pointed around to the ghost buildings that were no longer there. "Now right about yonder,"
he said, "is where the hotel stood. The church was over
there. There were four houses here. For years we raised tobacco up here. And we had trees, a grove of giant trees, just
about yonder. But we grubbed them. Old Opp who was here
would grub them. He'd dig a tree up all by himself. He
grubbed them out by their roots."

Now *all* was W-Hollow.

"It's like coming to a ghost town," I said.

I thought of the 1000 acres of W-Hollow: all neat as a pin.
"There's a lot of land to keep cleared and mowed," I said.

He agreed.

"This is a cattle hangout here," he said of the pasture
where the cabin was. "They like this spot. They got a salt

lick and everything." We were driving away, into the gloom of the attending forest. "There's a wild apple tree," he pointed. "We come here and get wild apples. We got 'em down in the hollow, too. Sometimes we get as many as ten bushels."

He steered the car through a slight clearing in the trees, a clearing hardly more than a wide lane. He stopped, looked around, contemplating all of it.

"You ought to have seen this place three years ago," he said. "We just got it underbrushed."

It looked like a huge and beautiful park. I said so. "You have to keep after it every year or it reverts, doesn't it?" I asked.

He pointed amongst the trees. "See my pond down yonder? Had to build it in back. Couldn't put it in front," he said. "The back of our house is down there somewhere. This through here on the ridge is nothing but rock cliff. When I was a boy I slept under that rock ledge many times, even in winter. I'd be out hunting. I never knew someday I'd own it."

We stared at another pastureland. "There were woods here once," he said. "But the timber was cut off the place before I bought it. I could never have afforded to buy it with timber on it."

Farther along the lane, he paused and pointed into the shadows of the forest.

"There," he said, "a giant house once stood. When I was a little boy my mother and father raised potatoes here. All around that house. I think I can show you where the old well was. My goodness, I remember this old house. It remembers fine. There was a big post right about here. An enormous

gate was over there. Lord, I used to plow right through here
myself."

"Do you come up here often?" I said.

"Oh, every once in awhile," Jesse Stuart said. "I never can
get to see enough of it. See where that bunch of old trees are?
That's where the well used to be. We had it filled up so the
cattle wouldn't fall into it. It was some well! It went straight
down—eighty feet, sixty feet of it through solid rock!"

"You've developed your own national forest, haven't
you?"

"Yes," he said. "You might say that. I keep everybody out
except picnickers who don't destroy. Once in awhile they
come up here. Most go to amusement parks that have rides."

And do not have the magic of the windflower.

He put the car in gear. We eased along the widened lane,
still beside the forest where the long-ago house had been.
Each tree possessed a private memory for him.

"My mother used to dress us up," he said, "and bring us up
here from the hollow. We'd sit by that big old deserted
house, waiting and looking to see if any ghosts went in or
out. My mother would get to talking about these ridges, who
had ridden them years before, and all the young lovers that
had lived and loved in the hills. She told us of the house and
the people that had been in it. I later wrote that story. Yeah,
I later wrote that story, 'Walk in the Moonshadows.' "

The car began to move a little faster to outdistance the
memories.

"This is the land," he said, with melancholy, "that is almost
a virgin area for writing stories for tomorrow—if they're
well-written, Dick, and if they are told with moods. Moods
in a story are awfully important."

We drove along a moment in rare silence.

Finally I said, "You're creating a sort of Eden here, aren't you? Do you get that feeling?"

"I'm not sure," he said honestly. "It takes somebody from the outside to come in and look at it fresh. See that ridge over there? I've got a novel about it. The old man that lived there had horsehairs on the outside of his shack for certain winds to blow and make music on the horsehairs for him. He believed in everything! He was just the opposite of my dad. Neither one of them were educated men. Dad believed in exterminating everything that he didn't believe was useful to man. The old man believed the opposite: that everything was put on the earth for a purpose. They couldn't stand one another. They could just look at one another and get their danders up. My dad despised him. He despised my dad. . . ."

More silence. Then:

"Look there, Dick, " he said. "Sheep fence. I once had five hundred sheep here. That's when we needed sheep fences. But the dogs destroyed the sheep farm. We have had miles and miles of woven wire fences. I'd like to know myself how many miles of fences we got over these one thousand acres. The real old fences are beautiful, aren't they? These fences here, along this ridge, we built in the thirties. I had three men working with me on small wages. I was only earning one hundred dollars a month back then. I bought this big parcel of the farm here, and selling stories to *Collier's* helped me pay for it. I sold three stories to them for five hundred apiece. That was a fortune! I ought to do a lecture sometime on the economics of being a writer. You should, too, Dick. People don't know the troubles we have. They look upon all of us as rich."

More silence, then a few pastures later:

"I bought my cows from the man who owned the Blue Grass Cattle Farm," he said. "The bull came from Ohio State University. I got some cows from the University of Kentucky, too. Herefords. That old cow over yonder is getting on in years, but I keep 'em a long time. Your horned herefords are your big cattle, your big breeding cattle."

He steered around a calf that gave us stares.

We were riding out in the open. The great valley of W-Hollow down beyond the tree line spread out before us like unpopulated wilderness. If you were a stranger you would swear the land was deserted. But Jesse Stuart knew where every house and farm structure was. He had memorized his land.

Of the pasture we were crossing, he said, "We farmed this, too." It was a sloping pasture, not as steep as the others had been, but slanty enough. "We raised the awfullest lot of corn you ever saw here," he said. "That hill down there, see it? We have had men go with scythes to clear her. We used machinery to keep the rest neat, but down there you have to go in by hand."

He pointed to a fencerow.

"Right along here," he said, "the road used to be that I walked to high school when I taught there. It came here from around that ridge yonder. I'd come this way, sit under the trees and write. I've written things sitting along here that have sold to big magazines. There used to be a log there I always sat on. I wrote a great portion of *Man with a Bulltongue Plow* right in there and where the cattle are now. That was when I was county school superintendent, walking back and forth to Greenup every day. Boy, I wonder how

many times my father walked along this road, going to
Greenup to work on the railroad section? This road was our
only way out of the hollow then. It was all we had between
here and the rest of the world. It was a long walk, but my
mother thought nothing of walking it, either. My sisters
walked it. My brother walked it. The whole family walked
in, every season of every year, twelve months a year."

"In a way," I said, "you're fortunate. You can accumulate
here all the odds and ends and moods and mementos of your
yesterdays and keep them intact, can't you?"

"That's right," he agreed.

Yet, the thought saddened as well as pleased the two of us.

"Does this look as beautiful from the air?" I said.

"Oh my goodness, yes," he said, perking up again.

"This is the prettiest country. Over there is where my
sheep slept, right in the highest place. I'd stop and look at the
sheep and talk to them. Now, look down there. See that little
hill that looks as round as a persimmon? I used to plow
around and around and around that little hill, making one
continuous row, winding all the way up to the top of it. I
wrote of this one time in high school; it was later published
in a school textbook. That other ground over yonder, about
twenty acres, I plowed in two weeks during a spring vaca-
tion. I told my Dad I could do it with a young pair of mules.
He didn't believe me, but I did it all right. I plowed, har-
rowed, and laid it off and planted it. I felt if I didn't do it I
would never be more defeated in my life. I went after things
that way. I went after Latin and got it. I went after algebra
and got it, too. I figured if I could get algebra, the land
would be easy."

We lingered along the fence, looking about us. Our backs
were to Ohio, the industrial river we couldn't see, and the

civilization that fermented there in gloom. We faced south to wilderness, and a kind of tranquillity descended upon us. Jesse Stuart brimmed with memories that kept tumbling out.

"I've walked this so many times," he said, "and I've written so many poems here. This once was in brush, but fires have burned it clear, and all the timber has been cut. It's just wasteland, really, this patch. We cleared it everywhere we could reach. Now we just keep her picked up and let her sit."

After a moment he said:

"We've raised some awfully good corn here."

After another moment, he said:

"The prettiest farm in Greenup County . . ."

I looked about. "Are those some of the gullies your father filled in?" I said.

He nodded.

"Yep," he said. "There's where the gullies were. Look over yonder, Dick. See those apple trees? *I* set 'em. I set every one of them. My mother and I came up here one time and we looked at the fruit on the tree and I wrote a poem, Dick; I wrote a poem right there. I mean, there was my mother and there was the apple tree. *She* was a tree that *I* had been born of. I wrote that poem right there!"

And many others of her:

> *I shall not speak soft words with stilted phrase*
> *To one who has worked all her live-long days*
> *In furrowed fields and in the open spaces,*
> *But I shall sing of her in plowman's phrase. . .*

We moved on.

We bounced down again into the hollow and the road. We

were heading back to the house. Again the hills were tight around us.

"You like the way the fences are creosoted, Dick?" Jesse Stuart asked, the board fencing drifting by us. "Old Charlie creosotes them. He could swim in creosote and not be bothered. He's the only one around here who could do it. My dad used to, but only old Charlie is left that does."

More silence, then:

"Look yonder, Dick. Quick. My goodness, that's a big woodpecker. Looky at the way he's going after that tree. You don't see many woodpeckers that big, big as a crow! They're pileated woodpeckers." He indicated the approaching meadow and where the house was. "This meadow," he said, "and the sides of the hills. We've farmed most of it, one time or another." He glanced at some trees. "I'm going to have to cut those scrubby pines out of there someday. They're getting too close to the road. We'll put those pines right in that low place there by the ditch, put some twigs back this way, and when the water sloshes down, carrying sediment, it'll catch in the pines and stay there. It will fill right up. That's the way we do land around here. We work with nature, not against it."

"Does the creek run out much?" I said.

The little creek, hardly more than a trickle, played tag with the road through the narrow hollow.

"Oh, Lord, yes," said Jesse Stuart. "You should see that creek run out after a heavy rain."

"Why is this area called W-Hollow?" I said, as he stopped the car in front of his house.

"Because," said the poet with country logic, "it is in the shape of a W. Part of the W winds into Greenup; most of it runs around here." He was waving his arms every which way to indicate directions. I accepted his explanation.

"Naomi Deane and I," he said, getting out of the car, "have lived here going on thirty-one years. And *I've* lived here all my life."

"And traveled around the world," I said.

"And always come back," he said. He looked at the trees that surrounded his home. "See that big white oak there?" he said. "I've a good notion to put my television antenna on it. If it was on that tree, I could probably get Columbus. I'd like to get another television channel. All we get now are the ones from West Virginia. Wouldn't it be wonderful if I could get a Cincinnati station? I get the biggest kick out of watching that Pete Rose play baseball. He's a pistol. He's all right, too. He plays to *win*."

I followed him into the house. Deane, coming smiling from the kitchen, said, "Well, boys, how was your trip?"

"I'm trying to figure out," I said, meaning only kindness, "whether it is real or unreal. What you have here seems unreal compared to some of the other hollows."

The look in Deane's eyes said she understood.

The look in Jesse Stuart's eyes said the same.

I felt better.

We were friends who could be honest. That was awfully important to all three of us.

ELEVEN

FLY from Cincinnati to the Huntington-Ashland Airport, located on a hilltop, look down at the rumpled start of mountains, and there you can see them: the trim red barn and the tiny box-like white frame cottage sitting in a lonely pasture atop one of the hills. Regulars who fly that way know that the next adventure is the airplane bouncing over that bump in the sky caused by warm air exhausted from the Ashland industries. I've looked down myself many times at the lone cottage and lone barn atop the hill. I never knew the cottage was Jesse Stuart's writing hideaway when visitors to the hollow get too much for him. But then I sat with him in that cottage—so far from everything but the wind and the sound of an occasional airplane getting up courage to land at the airport.

The trip from his home in W-Hollow had not taken long: ten or fifteen minutes. We could have got there quicker but Jesse Stuart had stopped to memorize a tree. That can take time. Deane had walked out to the car from their home. The day was sunny and bright, a beautiful hollow day when everything seemed right.

"Ask her," Jesse Stuart had said, "Dick, go on and ask her. Maybe she knows the answer." Without waiting for me, he said to Deane, "He's trying to figure out whether I'm a teacher who writes or a writer who teaches."

Deane didn't hesitate.

"He's a writer who teaches," she smiled. "He *likes* to teach, but he *has* to write."

"My goodness," said Jesse Stuart, "I'm glad I'll never get to the point where I have to choose between writing and teaching, though. But I'll never stop writing—*period*. They can retire you from teaching, but not writing. I'll never stop writing and neither will you, Dick. I can tell."

"How can we?" I said. "When you like to write, what else is there to retire to?"

He nodded. "I've had teaching," he said, "and I've had farming. I'm out of farming now for physical reasons. If I could, I would be out doing a lot of work on my farm, but the way my heart is, I can't. My heart is what stops me." He looked around the meadow in the hollow before he climbed into the car. "Dick, I've done more work than anybody I ever hired to work here. I like to work. I *like* it! I like turning over ground. I like to plant, to sow, and to see the stuff come up. Farming is the greatest thing. It does wonders for people who have mental troubles, too. Give them a piece of ground, let them work the soil, and let them see things grow."

"A sense of continuity," Deane said. "Well, you boys, come back in time for lunch."

She went back into the house, and we started for the cottage.

"A sense of continuity," said Jesse Stuart. "She's right. I'm not enough of a doctor to know, but I do know *that* works. I'll tell you something else, Dick. People used to ask me how I did as much as I did. Well, here's the secret." He steered the little car up the lane and up the winding rocky road that led to the lonely hilltop pasture. "I've worked with the land enough to make a balance to make me want to write. And to teach. You see the variety? The land gave me rest when I worked it—*head* rest. The land made me create. This is resurrection here, all around us: the trees, the plants, the flowers. It's all beauty: clean air and stars and blue sky."

Later, when we were settled in the cool of the cottage, I said, "What turned you to writing in the first place?"

He sat at the kitchen table, drumming his fingers. He was a restless writing man. He said, "I just think it was born in me. I got some encouragement from my English teacher in Greenup High School. She was Mrs. R. E. Hatton and she gave me a book of Robert Burns to read. I carried that book everywhere, reading it. She let us decide what topics we wanted to write about. Isn't that the important thing? She left it to us. That's what started me. I did some good ones for her, too. One of them was 'Nest Egg' that's now being used in textbooks. I wrote that when I was in high school, sixteen years old."

"But suppose you hadn't had a teacher like that?" I said. But I knew the answer and he did not fail me.

"I would have gone on writing anyway," he said. That is the way writers are. "I know I would have. But I've sure been lucky. I ran into another dandy teacher at Lincoln University. He was Harry Kroll. I have all of his books down there on one of the shelves at home. He turned us loose, too. Sometimes he'd even leave the class to go watch a baseball game. While he was teaching there, he had two books published. He said to me, 'Stuart, you won't be a short-story writer.' I wanted to tell him I wanted to be a novelist, but all I

said was 'Mr. Kroll, why won't I be?' He said I was too scat-
terbrained. He looked at me and said, 'Stuart, you're going to
be a poet.' One of the best teachers I ever had. But he missed
in his judgment about short-story writing."

"How?" I said.

"He was of the school that believed a short story needed a
plot," said Jesse Stuart. "You know, a twist at the end or
something. I didn't believe in that. In Greenup High School
I'd found this book of short stories by de Maupassant, read
every one, and loved them all. He didn't use plots. He used
slices from life, sometimes only an idea. That's what gave me
a bigger concept of the short story than my university
teacher had."

Each writer has his own theories which to him seem valid.
In some areas, Jesse Stuart and I agreed on writing tech-
niques. In other areas we didn't. But this was no quarrel between us. We each write the way that is most comfortable
for us. When creative writing becomes a chore, not worth
the effort, is when a creative writing instructor who can't
write his own way out of a paper bag demands that his students be of this or that writing school. Jesse Stuart and I both
agreed with that: such instruction kills writing dead.

A cow looked in the kitchen door at us, chewed its cud;
then because it had no interest in the problems of writers, it
wandered elsewhere in search of its own reality. Jesse Stuart
had, only the day before, suffered through the reality of an
infected tooth and a trip to the dentist's chair. But he was
feeling chipper again, nervous as a cat because he has energy
to burn, but chipper nonetheless. The poet is a restless man.
His restlessness is cosmic.

"Do you write whether you are sick or well?" I said.

"I've written when I didn't feel too good," he said. "But not when I'm real sick. Man is prone *not* to write, you know. You get a man that goes to the typewriter every single day and you've got yourself a real writer. Some people can spend eight straight hours at the typewriter, But I just can't bring myself to it. I break the day up. I'll write just so much, revise just so much, and so on."

"Do you technically work about four to six hours a day, concentrating on it?" I said.

He nodded. "But," he said, "I have written ten hours a day."

"That's a lot of physical effort alone," I said.

"Did my own typing, too," he said. "Created right on the typewriter."

"Some writers say they can't do it that way," I said. "They have to brood a lot, but they do it other ways."

"I can't brood," said Jesse Stuart. "I've got to get her all out of my system."

To picture Jesse Stuart in this hidden cottage, cut off from the world of men, exhausting himself at his typewriter was easy for me to do. There is a momentum to writing. And, in addition, there are deadlines. The professional writer—not the dreamer awaiting the magic wand of inspiration—is aware of this momentum and these deadlines. I could picture this country poet, sitting at his typewriter, aching to quit, aching to go out and stroll the woods he loves, but sitting before that infernal machine and writing word after word after word after word. Soon a page is done. Then, another is done. A professional writer may be inspired, but he does not wait for inspiration. He *forces* it to come—and it does. Jesse Stuart is that kind of professional writer. What hurts most are not the pages which seem to type so slowly but the writer's back and typing hands. They physically hurt with exhaustion. To write for hours at a stretch is to wrestle that angry bear we writers call the muse. Many was the time Jesse Stuart got up from his typewriter, dazed, hardly aware of where he was, rubbed his eyes, and stepped outside wanting fresh air and reality. This is the way *real* writers are or they are not real writers. He and I agreed on this.

"Are you a fast or slow writer?" I asked him.

"The highest number of pages I've done in one day," he said, "was forty-two typewritten pages. That's a big day's work." The memory of it exhausted him all over again.

"Some writers turn out only a page a day," I said.

He nodded. "Right!" he said. "But I don't understand that. I'd never write that pokey way. That'd be a riddle to me. I have to turn loose like the blowing wind. I've got to get going. I've got to roll. I can't halt. When I get started, I'm like a flowing stream or a wind that blows over the meadow. I've got to *move*."

"Do you ever get hung up and worry about a word or sentence," I said. "Or do you bypass it and come back to it later?"

"Naw, Dick, I never hang up on a word. My goodness, if I can't find the word I want at that time, I just keep on going. I'll hang up when I revise. But I want to get the story down on paper first. I want to get the mood of the poem down. I can think about words later. It works that way for me, too," he added.

This is another reason I like him. He and I, though the things we write are different, approach writing the same way. Dawdling isn't the name of our writing game. But I

said, in fairness to the many other ways to exhaust yourself
on paper, "I write the same way, not waiting for the right
word to come before I can get on with the sentence. But I
have seen other writers stare at legal pads for hours, with
pencils poised, waiting for the right word to fly by so they
can proceed."

He peered at me.

"If I did that," he said, "I'd go crazy. I couldn't sit and
stare at a blank sheet of paper. I'd have wagons rolling on
that page and sky and everything. I'd have people walking
and talking on that page. I wouldn't wait around for a word
to set me free to write. I'd write! Listen, when I scribble in
longhand I make mistakes because I think faster than my
hand can move. I start leaving off letters of words and after
awhile '-ing's,' just putting part of a word down."

"Have you developed a kind of shorthand?" I said. *I* had.
But I have never developed the technique of transcribing it
later; it ends up lines of useless squiggles that seem intelligible
only at the time of making them.

"Isn't it strange you should ask that question," he said.
"Somebody asked me one time what course I'd missed that I
wished I had taken and I said shorthand. I wish I had it. I've
made notes that I couldn't read later, had to take 'em so fast."
That confession made me feel better; I was not alone. "If I
can get just a few words down on an idea, though," he went
on, "and get those words to remind me, I can go back
through every thought I had when I put those words down. I
don't have to put it *all* down. Why, I can show you note-
books that will throw you. One is a little fertilizer notebook
I've been writing in—oh, I don't know how many years. I
think I must have seventy-five notes in it for short stories. I
had it over in Greece with me."

"So you never worry about running out of things to write?" I said.

"I," he said, "don't think I can ever finish *all* I've got to write. People are always giving me ideas for books, ideas I can't use because there is no time."

"No worry about writer's block?" I said.

Writer's block: that terrible day a writer sits down to write and nothing comes: no words, no sentences, no paragraphs, no dialogue, no description—*nothing*. Some writers don't believe the animal called *writer's block* exists; they believe it is simply a way of avoiding the pain of writing.

"Now I won't say there isn't writer's block," he said, "because after the war when I came back here, something happened. I couldn't get into the swing of things. I had changed. But I got back into the movement. The stuff I wrote then was terrible stuff."

"Did any of it sell?"

"No," he admitted. "I've destroyed nearly all of it since. It was just no good."

I thought of the piles of scripts I had seen stored away in the nooks and crannies of the W-Hollow buildings. "You seem to keep a lot of stuff, too," I said. I was pleased that he did. I never throw anything away. Such writers are pack rats, fire hazards, but, somehow, efficient.

"And you'd better watch what you do throw away," Jesse Stuart warned. "I had a story one time called 'The Slipover Sweater.' No, it wasn't called anything; Naomi Deane titled it later. It laid around up here four years. My wife looked at it one day and said, 'This a good story, Jesse.' The pages of it had actually turned brown, had weathered. So I told her I'd revise it and retype it. Wasn't much revision needed. Sent it to *Woman's Day* and they paid me the highest I'd ever been paid till then for a story. They paid me a thousand dollars. It's a wonder I hadn't thrown the story away. That thousand dollars came in mighty handy because right then we were needing money. Today the story is in a Scott-Foresman text-book. It's been in that textbook for years. Yet, I didn't think it was worth anything. Let's be frank about this. A writer doesn't know his own worth quite often."

"How do you pick your markets?" I said. Translated to the non-writer, this means how do you decide to which mag-azine you'll send a story in the hopes they'll buy it.

"I never write for a market," he said. "I write my own way. *Then*, I look over the markets and try to see which is nearest to what I've written. That book I mentioned before called *Writer's Market* is a big help. Do you know it?"

"Yes," I said. "The Rosenthals in Cincinnati publish it."

"That's the best market book published in the United States," the poet said.

"Did you know Aron Mathieu from Rosenthal's?" I said.

"I met him once at the University of Indiana," said Jesse Stuart. "I was teaching a writing course and he came out. He lectured. That was in 1940. I haven't seen him since."

Point is, some writers don't mingle with others of their trade, and this is the way Jesse Stuart is. Aron Mathieu, on the other hand, mingled with them all, but this made sense. He was then editor of *Writer's Digest*, which the Rosenthals published from their family printing business at 22 East Twelfth Street, Cincinnati. He and Jesse Stuart have much in common. They are both children pretending to be grown-up. In their professions—writing and editing—they *are* about as mature as you could want professionals to be, but each is possessed of an enthusiasm for life that children have.

Neither Aron Mathieu nor Jesse Stuart has outgrown this enthusiasm. Each morning, it seems to me, they are surprised by
sunrise just as, each night, they are awed by the first star. In a
way it's just as well that their paths have not crossed much.
Each would have exhausted the other with joy.

"He's still at Rosenthal's," I told the poet of his friend. "He
still works there because he says a person should retire *to*
something and not *from* something, and he can't find anything to retire to."

"He's doing a marvelous job," said Jesse Stuart. "You'd be
surprised at how many of those *Writer's Market*s I've sold.
That's *one* book I help sell! Why? Because people come to
me and worry me about where to send what they've written.
I tell them to get the market book and that they won't miss
on it. One of my second cousins got a copy, used it, and
today he's sold up to nine books. He got with Putnam
through *Writer's Market*."

"Did you ever have an agent?" I said.

"In the early days, yes," he said. "I had an agent and a
good one. She was one of the finest agents in the business. But
she cracked up and became a mental. Ed Kuhn can tell you
about her. The last time I talked with him, he said she was in
a mental institution. This girl sold my short stories. She got
me an awful lot of good contracts. Annie Laurie Williams
later sold one of my books to the movies. My first agent handled Truman Capote, Mary Aswell, and all of them. Mary
Aswell's husband was a vice-president at McGraw-Hill when
Ed Kuhn was an editor there."

"Did you ever have an article about writing published in
Writer's Digest?" I asked.

He shook his head no, puzzled.

"My goodness," he said, "I never *did* have any luck with them that way. I sent them an article once. I thought it was a good article. They turned it down. One of the hardest magazines to get into," he added, "is the *Kansas Quarterly* though."

He grinned.

"But I sent them the article *Writer's Digest* rejected," he said, "and they took it. *Kansas Quarterly* just grabbed it like that.

We talked about a half hour—gleefully—of the sly ways writers get at publishers. Each writer has many stories like this. We were, as we sat in his writing cottage atop the lonely hill, children at recess, figuring ways we could make hash of the process. We did not feel bad about doing this. In our small world it is the writer versus the publisher. In our world the publisher has the better chance of winning. It's his game. He can—and does—change the rules as he goes. Our victories are small by comparison, but our joy, by comparison, is great. Writers will be ever thus.

Then we talked of creative writing courses. We had mixed feelings about them.

Said Jesse Stuart: "A lot of those who attend should never be in the course. But they have to come and find out on their own, and they go away feeling better, I guess. I can't tell them that they—most of them—shouldn't be there. The other writers in the class do, though. For instance, there's this Jesse Stuart Workshop at Murray. For one thing, I wanted them to leave my name off of it and call it the Murray State University Workshop, but they named it after me anyway, and they let me run it my way. It's the only writing workshop I've ever run. I know when the students come in they're soon going to find out whether or not they can write. They're each on their own. I tell them that any kind of writing they want to try is fine with me, just so they put down something on paper. They don't know that the world is big and that writing is big. They just start writing. It's hard to tell what they end up with. They've turned in almost every kind of writing there is, and that way, I see some awfully good material."

"But other writing workshops?" I said.

He gazed helplessly at the pasture, saddened. "I worked at another one for a week," he said. "The difference was that they had men lecturing in—of all things!—Shakespeare! They had men lecturing in things that had nothing to do with creativity. At least, that's how I feel. But they had a fine journalism teacher. He got almost two hundred articles from that group that he considered publishable. He didn't have lectures. He had the people *writing!* I won't have lectures, either. What's the use of somebody coming in telling me about Romeo and Juliet? What has that got to do with the class writing? What has that got to do with creativity? Now I'm an English major myself, Dick, and I have the equivalent of a Ph.D. in English. I've taught English in college. I've taught it in high school. But English departments have nothing to do with creativity. Only journalism departments do."

"Do you think most high schools and colleges kill creativity?" I said.

I was thinking of my son taking freshman English at a university in Ohio. I looked over his assignments and what his teacher demanded. Most of it was nonsense. Had I taken my

son's course, I would have flunked it. Or been kicked out of
school for laughing in the lecture room at the methods used
to teach.

Jesse Stuart was on my side in this. "They kill creativity,"
he said. "They kill it. Let's be frank about that. They kill it. I
know places right now where friends of mine are teaching it
and they don't even know they're killing it. But I don't open
my mouth because how can I control it? I can't go in and tell
a Ph.D. to change his ways, can I? Over at Indiana University, I helped to save their creative writing course. They had
me in as just a minor figure but it ended up fine. There was a
teacher there who just wouldn't allow creativity to die. The
others running the course sort of stepped aside and let the
two of us take over. We had ourselves a fine time."

"I'm troubled," I said, "by what the kids are taught in the
name of 'creative writing.' "

"It's not creative writing," said Jesse Stuart. He had strong
feelings on this. "Dick, how many places can you go in high
school today where a teacher lets the student choose the subject to write about? When I taught high school, I let my kids
choose their own subjects. They ended up with choosing
good ones I would have never thought of. That way the class
was bigger than I was, it was as big as all of us in it. There
was one thing I made them understand. I'd tell them they
were all going to pass even if they didn't do much writing.
This relaxed them. I'd tell them the world is out there, all of
it. I'd say, 'Writing comes out of the air, so you better be
there to snatch it. Writing is *your* experiences. Tell me about
your experiences, tell me about people, tell me about yourself, tell me about some interesting character. There are all

kinds of interesting subjects. What did you do today? What did you do yesterday?' "

"And grammar?" I said.

"We forgot about grammar," he said. "Grammar comes second. Here's one idea I used. We would exchange papers. Each student would grade another's. They would find mistakes in grammar and in spelling. That taught them grammar and how to correct. I went over the papers after the kids were through with them. I always had the student who did the correcting put his name on the paper he corrected. In that class I had grammar two days a week, life and literature one day a week, memory work one day a week, and themes one day a week—and we never did get through each class by the time the bell rang! Now and then I'd get a frivolous student, monkeying around in class, and I'd tell him, with a smile 'cause I wasn't mad at him, 'Son, I believe you know what we're doing here, so if you'd like to take over the class today, go right ahead, and I'll sit down and be one of the students.' *That* would stop him."

"Did any ever accept your challenge?" I said.

"Had one boy who did," said Jesse Stuart, pleased. "And my goodness, he got up and did a pretty good job of it, too. He told them to read their themes. I said, 'I've got one here, let me read.' I used to read my stories with my students because they had good judgment. We had a real good time that day. They'd read stories of mine that later made old *Collier's*."

"Your first critics, huh?" I said.

The word *critics* bothered him. He peered at me, rubbed his crew cut, and said, "If I was put up, I wouldn't get a vote from the critics. Do you know where my votes would come from? From the people, the readers! Schoolteachers and farmers and men working on the railroad. But not from the critics. Critics can't make a living from their writing, but *I* can. The books the critics go nuts over often don't sell. Critics like *literary* things. Well, most literary books don't sell, but mine do."

We sat atop the hill, listened to an airplane inching in slow-motion across the sky, and thought about New York.

"There seem to be so many self-perpetuating literary circles," I suggested. "They're killing literature and everyone not in their little club."

"You and I don't belong to that circle, Dick."

I nodded.

To belong and be praised, even for the wrong reasons, would be a pleasant experience each of us would love to have—at least once. But, we agreed in the wilderness, we were not members of the club.

"You're a normal man, aren't you, Dick?"

"I don't write about homosexuality," I said.

"Well, there you are. That's all they know," Jesse Stuart complained. "That's the way books are now. Now that's the way the theater is, too. I wonder about most of those hotshot New York writers. How can a woman find a normal man among them?"

He drummed his fingers on the table with impatience.

"Isn't it strange," he said, "that there's something wrong with so many of the artists? Now mind you, they can't help it because they can't help being what they are, but Lord! the stuff they're putting out to the public! I never saw anything like it."

"I was reading the other day," I said, "where there's hardly a market for humor any more."

He nodded.

"I mentioned that same thing to my class this summer," he said. "There's this one fellow, kind of a scholarly type, who has done two hundred and fifteen pages for an article on *my* humor. It's scholarly, but it's there. The thing is, you start out to write a story. If it turns out funny, fine. You're a humorist. On the other hand, it could turn out sad. Who knows?" he ended helplessly. Humor is too elusive.

"Do you find your characters suddenly saying things in your stories that they shouldn't?" I said, "as if they had developed minds of their own and got away from you?"

"Oh, my goodness, yes," he said. "But you put so much of yourself into every character. As a writer, you've got to be many people. You've got to be all of them in your story."

I told him of the time a lady had interviewed me after seeing one of my plays. She had asked which character I was. She was irritated when I had told her I had been all of them —because I had created all of them.

"Right!" he agreed. "But they never understand that, do they, Dick?"

"I wonder," I said, "if you were starting out over again, in this moment in time the way the markets are, if you would have succeeded as a writer? Or would you have ended up superintendent of a school system somewhere and out of it?"

That question troubled him. "I'm not sure," he said. "I started at the right time. Time helped make me. It was a magazine world then, but it's not now. I wrote for magazines and loved every minute of it. In those days, people *read* magazines."

He walked to the door, a huge poet-farmer-dreamer of a man, stood there, his back to me, looking out at the wilderness his magazine stories had accumulated for him. Each tree was a paragraph written, mailed, sold. Each blade of grass was a comma, waving in the hilltop breeze. The magazine world had been beautiful. But that afternoon on the hilltop, its beauty was a faintly remembered thing, like trying to conjure up the face of a girl who passed you years before on a busy street and smiled with love at you.

"But writing took me over, don't you see?" Jesse Stuart was saying to me. " 'The way the twig is bent,' however that goes. It was the way this one boy wrote me up in his thesis: come hell or high water I was headed for my destiny and nothing stood in my way. But why are we so vain, Dick? What makes us writers that way?"

"It is a vain assumption," I agreed, feeling the sadness he felt, "to sit down and write something and to presume someone will want to read what was written. It's a vain assumption that we have something to say."

Silence.

After the longest time, he said, almost to himself, "But if there had been no magazines . . ."

He didn't have to say the rest. Both of us knew.

"But there were," I said. "There were."

He looked at me, cheerful again.

"Oh yes," he said. "Oh, my goodness, yes. . . ."

TWELVE

I THINK," said Jesse Stuart, "a man ought to go armed. I really do. I'm almost a member of the Society of Friends when it comes to taking any kind of life, but I've thought this thing through: what would *I* do if it was my life or someone else's? Suppose he's out to get me for no reason? I'd be justified shooting him. I couldn't forget it the rest of my days, though," he added.

We sat in the car by the Greenup courthouse, the back side of which faces the Ohio River; memories of Greenup's yesterdays flooded back to the poet.

"I've been in a situation right around here," he said, "where I thought I was going to have to shoot a man. A man hit me for no reason and he threatened Naomi Deane. I carried a pistol after that for I don't know how long. I carried two. It was over school business we fussed. I was superintendent here. Yes, I carried a pistol." He gazed at the river, troubled. "I have three scars today on my head from it."

"Have things settled here?" I asked.

"Oh, yes," he said. "Time heals everything. That was back in 1938. But it made *Time* magazine and everything else around. They don't like to be reminded of it around here or think that it even happened, but it sure did. Dick, look what

I've gone and done. I've gone on from that time and published more books. Even then I had three or four published. I've had nearly three dozen books published. And the fellow that hit me served on three different occasions in the penitentiary. One of his sons has been there once or twice. His other son has been there once. So that's their record. And that's mine: nearly three dozen books. Let the people judge.

"But he was protected here by his party. The Democratic party used him. In the thirties around here we had a kind of Democratic party dictatorship. And they *freed* him! He said he'd never do any more mean things. He said he regretted what he had done. So they up and freed him. They even made him constable. When Naomi Deane and I were married, tempers around here were still pretty mean against me. But she married me in the face of it. The mood of the county was slow to change back in those days. Today it would be a passing wind and be over. Today people don't like to remember or even think about unpleasant things. They have no sense of history, here in Greenup—or anywhere else for that matter."

He stared at a wizened old-timer sitting on a wooden bench in front of where a side-street store had once been. I didn't ask if Jesse Stuart knew the old man. I was certain he did. Greenup—town and county—isn't that big. People know everybody, the good and the bad and all of the rest that sits there stewing in between.

"I was over here at a reunion," he said, "last Sunday—or when? A Sunday a week ago, I think. One of my first cousins was there. He is almost my age. We went to school together, played baseball together, and everything. Swam in the river, hunted wild bees, fox-hunted together. We sat around the reunion talking about the one-room school up there in Plum Grove and pokeberry ink and all of it. I wrote a story about making pokeberry ink, how it stained your fingers. I wish I could have held onto more of those memories so I could get them down on paper. I wrote about pluto water. I wrote about those things down here in Greenup in high school, too. I wished I had saved all that material, but I didn't."

Greenup, of course, is still there, but Riverton isn't; Greenup swallowed her up. About one mile of emptiness used to separate the two villages, but the emptiness filled up with houses, and there you are.

At W-Hollow an important piece of Riverton remains. It is in one of the rooms where the poet writes. It is that cubby-holed thing mail used to be stuffed into till natives came by for what had been mailed to them. In that thing was one cubbyhole that had belonged to the Stuarts. It was there Jesse Stuart's first literary checks were stuffed, awaiting the poet to come by and fetch them.

"It was an octagon-walled post office," Jesse Stuart recalled. "Eight-sided. Awfullest-looking building you ever saw. Locust trees grew around it. That's where I first started sending out manuscripts. When I'd get a check back, I'd open the envelope and show the postmaster. She used to say, 'Jesse, you're the beatin'est boy I ever saw. Imagine, fifty dollars for some writing! The postmaster was really postmistress. She was a lady, a fine lady. . . ."

U.S. 23, which goes east-west in a wiggly way on the Kentucky side of the Ohio River, bypasses Greenup. Now Greenup itself slumbers. No cars whiz through on streets that Jesse Stuart once helped pave. The courthouse attracts some, but most are locals.

"Riverton," said Jesse Stuart, "used to be a pretty good size, but Greenup would take a little bit of it, just kept cutting away at her. And there used to be two railroads going through here. Now there's only the C&O. There used to be the Eastern Kentucky Railroad. The little EK had a terminal out toward the Ohio River. It had a track that went right down to the river barges. A little old steam locomotive used to chug up and down those tracks along the river bank. The EK would take stuff from the barges and lug 'em out into the mountain hollows. It ran close to the turnoff to Plum Grove cemetery. You can still see the old highline, but the tracks are all gone. And it brought stuff down from the hills, too. Coal mostly. Many a load has gone to Cincinnati from here. The C&O has an enormous depot here. They *had* two: one at Riverton and one at Greenup. Now the trains don't even stop here any more."

To live by the river is to be *of* the river. Jesse Stuart's brother-in-law has a boat on the Ohio River now. It's the *Laura VI*, named after his wife. On mellow summer evenings when the Ohio Valley gets stuffy hot—not a breeze stirring and the stands of trees are like tinder, waiting to explode—the Stuarts and their kin go out on this boat to where a cool twilight breeze is. They take overnight trips upstream, beyond the grimy complexes of Ashland and Huntington, seek out a little creek that empties into the river, go up her a ways, then tie up for the night. Said Jesse Stuart, "If you play with the river long enough, sooner or later, you know every little stream that goes into it."

"When you were a kid," I said, "did you ever have a john-boat on the river?"

Johnboats? Wooden, crude, nailed-together, awkward but

seaworthy craft a man rowed, sometimes pulling his shanty-
boat to a new location because a farmer chased him off, or
sometimes checking the catch from his illegal trotlines strewn
across the river.

"Oh, yes," said Jesse Stuart. "We used to have one all the
time. Back at Lincoln Memorial University, we'd go on pic-
nics, and I'd row or pole the boat along. They'd put one man
to a boat, load 'em up with picnickers, and I used to have a
good load in mine, but I could pass up all the other boats
easy. I used to do that down at school."

"Did you ever ride the rollers the sternwheel riverboats
made for their wake?" I said.

"No," he said. "Never did that. But I remember one lake
by Middlesboro, Kentucky. They put a dam in there. That
was some lake. I would sure like to go back there some day.
Water as clear as crystal, Dick. It was back up in the mountains, no houses, no coal mines, nothing. Just a beautiful lake,
two miles long. It was beautiful, really beautiful back there."

We looked at the Ohio River, funny-colored from the stuff
all the chemical plants and cities upstream dumped into it.
We looked at it and said nothing. Once the Ohio River had
been a sweet-water stream, too, but that was back there, it
seemed, before anybody's time. I had written of this stretch
of the Ohio River valley before. In the book *Ohio, Personal
Portrait of the Seventeenth State*, I had said:

To those of you who seek only chamber of commerce ver-
biage and/or poetic beauty, fair warning. Things will not
improve too much in this wonderful river valley between
Ironton and Steubenville. To be sure, some towns may de-
light you with elegance, but many others have been too

thunderstruck by industry. Just as on a murky day the
fumes that trailer trucks spew linger in the air above the
expressway, so in places does smoke hover over this industrial complex we call the Upper Ohio Valley. Here are
not history's gentle valleys of yesteryear, where throughout the empty land birds sang songs to the west wind's
moan. Here, instead, is a hard-muscled cash box. From this
dynamic valley come the chemicals and ores which the rest
of us, lolling about some less sooty town, need, if we are to
exist. This is the valley of hard truths and men who are not
afraid to sweat. Coal does not voluntarily fly from the guts
of the hills. Chemicals do not blend themselves—unseen,
in distant kitchens. So do not seek pastoral beauty here.
Accept this valley for the truth it represents. Thus, while
the villages of this grimy place may not get rave notices, its
people and its industries do. Anyway, if pastoral beauty
were rampant throughout the land, the land would be silent. America would never have happened. So let the Iron-
tons and the Steubenvilles gather grime. If these people
went elsewhere and if each industry shut its door, the valley again would be clean. But when you ran out of gas,
there wouldn't be any more. . . ."

Jesse Stuart was of this valley of hard truths as well as of
the hollows back there beyond the sootfall and the grime.
After high school he had worked in the steel mills. He himself had tasted that clangorous world of redhot metals and
coals. We sat in his car, watching the river and the industrial
smog, and he was saying:
    "I became a striker—" (this was after high school in
Greenup) "that's a blacksmith helper at the mills. An old man

got ahold of me there. Boy, he was a first-class tramp. But he
was also a first-class blacksmith, one of the best. He weighed
two hundred and forty pounds. He wore a little leather skull-
cap. On his broomstick legs, he looked like a barrel. He told
me, 'I'll make something out of you as a striker.' I didn't
know then that a man could become an artist with a sledge-
hammer, swinging it. He showed me how to hit. We had a
contest at the fairs with our hitting. Us strikers would go to
the fairs and hit the thing with a wooden mallet to make the
bell up there clang. It was hard to ring them. Boys from the
country would come in, real giants, and they couldn't put it
halfway up to the bell. Well, this blacksmith said he would
make me a winner—and he did, too! There's a trick to it,
in the way you hit. He showed me the trick. I never told it
to anybody. Years afterward, I went to the Greenup fair and
rang it forty-five times! Other folks couldn't get it to ring
once. I rang it forty-five times straight. I walked away from
there with a hatful of cigars—they paid off in cigars—
and I didn't even smoke back then. I wrote it up. It turned
up in *Boy's Life* magazine called 'A Winner at the Fair.'
That old man was some blacksmith, Dick. He said, 'I'll make
a man out of you.' He'd throw his blacksmith tools out, making me go fetch them. That's the way he trained me. I got
training with two sledgehammers: one eight pounds, one
twelve pounds. I got real good training from him."

Something bothered the poet. He fingered another recollection before passing it along.

"Before I went to the blacksmith shop," he said, "I worked
with this air hammer. You'd have to put these cold bars in
there to measure the width of the hot bars—and you're
bringing them down with that air hammer. Boy, that was

dangerous! I was off one night and they brought in another man, a fine man, but he was a greenhorn and he got himself killed at my job. I had training in using the air hammer; he hadn't. You had to keep the pin by your side because that hammer can knock her out. Sometimes flying 'em clear across the shop. This fellow didn't hold the air hammer right. The pin went right through him. I'll never forget the blood on that dirt floor. We took shovels, covered it over, but it kept seeping right on through. . . ."

Before that, Jesse Stuart, while working for a contractor paving the Greenup streets, had seen other young people enter the high school. He was making three dollars for a ten-hour day, mixing cement, and he was only fifteen years old. That high school in Greenup was a magnet. The five miles between his home in the hollow and the high school meant little. High schooling meant the most. So he entered the school—a ten-mile trek each day—and started on his way. Those were sweet days to recollect. But Greenup is in hard-nosed country, where making it isn't duck soup.

"We've got several here that have got jobs somewhere and farm at home," said the poet of the population. "They work at a farm and they work at public work. It's hard to make a living here farming, Dick. Farming, like in Ohio flat land, has gone big-time. Illinois is the same: big farms that are big operations. So are Kansas and Iowa and the rest. Farmers hereabouts can't compete, raising corn and selling it, with the farmers from the flat land of Ohio where they get one hundred and twenty-five bushels an acre."

"The small farmer is dying?" I said.

"He's dead," said Jesse Stuart. "He's like the little stores they used to have here in Greenup. This one store here—

the Applegates—joined up with the chains. Another one here did, too. Had to."

I noted one little shop with the sign: MARY STUART DRESS SHOP.

"Relation?" I said.

He rubbed his chin, sorting out the comings and goings of the clan. "Yep," he said finally. "She was a Pennington and she married a Stuart. We're related both ways. I'm a fourth Pennington. I taught her daughter here in high school. They had one child, separated, she never married again. Ran that store. A *fine* lady, a very fine lady."

"Would a shop like hers make money in Greenup?" I said.

"She didn't get rich," said Jesse Stuart, "but she did all right. She educated her daughter with that shop. She sent her daughter to college."

"Do most hang out here at the courthouse?"

"The drug store is where you'll find 'em," he said. "Why, it's the center of town."

"How's the sheriff here?"

"A fine man, Dick. Why, I even voted for him, but I didn't think he would get elected. This is a Democratic county. But he's a good sheriff. In his younger days, he was a street fighter. He cleaned house back then. He'd fight them all over the streets of South Shore, Kentucky, and Portsmouth, Ohio. When he goes out, they get arrested. He's that kind. And he's a good family man and a good citizen. A false alarm went off in the sheriff's office the other morning before you got here; it was the burglar alarm from the bank, and there was the sheriff and his deputies surrounding the bank. The sheriff had his pistol at the door; he had it drawn. Why, he could have got anybody that came out of that bank.

He's got 'em before. The bank has been robbed once and he got the boy that did the robbing. The boy is in the pen now. I was down to that prison in western Kentucky. Sad. I never saw a place like that in my whole life."

Jesse Stuart drove slowly down the main street.

"Who ever does the things we used to do?" he said. "Who ever picks wild blackberries today to pay for their schoolbooks? Today the books are furnished. They don't *have* to be worked for." He thought about this a moment, then said, "Look what people miss when they don't have to work for things. I used to run with a bunch of boys that liked to consider themselves brave and tough. Well, these boys, tough and brave as they were, went out to pick blackberries to get money to buy schoolbooks with. We had a wagon and we had lard cans. There was a little sandy area we'd go to. It's called copperhead country, so not many others went. They were afraid of snakes. But that's where we'd go to pick berries. One of the boys got fanged by one of those copperheads and the other boy pulled off the snake and said, 'You won't bite my brother any more, you son-of-a-bitch!' and he hacked off the snake's head with his knife. Then he cut his brother's finger where the snake had bit and sucked blood. Put a handkerchief around it, tightened it, and the boy never even got sick. We went right on picking berries. That's how we were back in those days. If I had lived here in Greenup, I'd never have had adventures like that to write down."

We watched a school bus loaded with children go by. Jesse Stuart looked after it thoughtfully.

"Things are better now," he admitted. "Buses sure beat walking over the hills."

"What became of the fellows you picked berries with?" I said.

"I'm the only one of that bunch that finished high school," he said. The admission saddened him. "I played baseball with them. I fought with them. I wrestled with them. I swam with them. There was one amongst them who pitched sixteen innings. But that was when he was out there in the one-room Plum Grove school where the cemetery is now. We tied her up in the ninth and nobody on either side could get loose. We loved baseball."

"Why didn't they finish high school?"

"I don't know, Dick. Maybe they weren't sold on it or maybe they just didn't care about books. But there was some wild ones. There was this one that came off Beauty Ridge. He weighed two hundred and twenty pounds. I didn't know him but I heard tell of him. He rode a motorcycle all the time. We tried to get him to go to high school, but he wanted no part of it. He was older than the rest of us. Maybe that was why. But he'd attend every football and basketball game we played. He'd hurt the other side by crowing like a rooster. He was always mimicking animals—and he would have them fighting mad. When we'd go over to Portsmouth, we'd have ourselves a time. That's settled mostly by Kentuckians, you know, over there in that part of Ohio. There was one football game we had there that ended in a free-for-all. There was seven hundred of them from Portsmouth, all transplanted Kentuckians, and three hundred of us. Somebody cut the lights, lots of people got their teeth knocked out, and it was something. I don't know exactly how many teeth this boy from Beauty Ridge lost. All I know is, every

time somebody got up in the game to holler, he would hit
them right in the mouth. He liked to ride his motorcycle, like
I said. He'd do every kind of stunt on it, like put his feet on
the handlebars and go tearing through South Shore. Only,
one time he laid his motorcycle down, the engine was still a
little warm, and a copperhead crawled into the machine.
When he got back on his motorcycle, the copperhead started
crawling around, biting his leg. I don't know how many
times he was bitten. They rushed him to the hospital and the
next thing we saw was him racing around on his motorcycle,
crutches tied on in back. I don't know what he's doing now.
Whatever it is, he's probably good at it. He never had more
than an eighth grade education but he's a good worker, a real
good worker. I hope he's doing fine."

He mused, as he watched schoolchildren empty from the
bus.

"I think," he said, "they'd enjoy school more if it wasn't
handed to them so easy. I had to work like a mule for my
schooling. I worked like a mule, played football like a mule,
and loved every minute of doing it."

"But were there some you knew who didn't?" I said.

"Yes," he said truthfully. "Some came out of the back hills
and came down here to Greenup and turned into city boys.
They put on bow ties, dressed up, walked around a lot, and
left their old country heritage because they didn't want any
part of it. I remember three or four boys my age who did
that. But they never got anywhere."

"They eventually left Greenup, too?"

"Some did," he said. "Some stayed right here."

As we passed people whom Jesse Stuart certainly knew,
several seemed to look at the car as if he were a stranger.

Others waved. A few smiled. But I sensed something: Jesse
Stuart's love affair with his land and community was not exactly as pretty as old-fashioned valentines used to be. Maybe
he sensed this, too, because out of the blue he said:

"This is my base, Dick. But back in W-Hollow is my real
base. Only it all kind of runs together sometimes. Look at the
books I've got out of all of this. But that doesn't make me
some kind of legend. I'm like Jim Sparks here. I live in a
house, farm, do my writing chores, and build something from
scratch. When I see Jim on the streets, we stop together and
talk. He took care of his farm the same way I do mine. You
might say we saw the same dream: we saw the same land, the
same stars, and the same sky—and we both belonged to all
of it. I don't put myself above him. He's every bit as good as
I am. That's the way I feel about all my neighbors. They're
fine folks. But . . ."

He paused, weighed his words, then plunged ahead.

"But, Dick, listen a minute. I can tell from kind of innuen-
dos, some of the people hereabouts have different feelings
about me than I have about them. That road they paved out
to W-Hollow, for instance. They started saying around
Greenup that it was *my* road and was put in because *I* lived
there. But there are nineteen other people that live on that
hollow road, Dick. It's between two main highways and it
was the most traveled unpaved or unsurfaced road in the
county—or one of the most. I happen to think it was the
most traveled, but never mind. They thought I used pull to
get the road paved. One family here in town said was it true
it was going to be paved? That was when it hadn't been. I
said I sure hope so. After it started getting paved, everybody
along the hollow was tickled pink. But they keep saying *I* got

the road paved, *I* caused it to be improved. Some that live on other hollow roads, roads that haven't been paved yet, are mad at me. Maybe that's what you get when you write and get to be better-known. I don't know."

"Have most people around here read you?" I asked.

He frowned at the road ahead. We were approaching new U.S. 23, heading up County Road 2 that would lead us to the W-Hollow turnoff.

"Some of them have read me and some of them haven't," he said. "Some of them will come right out and tell you they won't buy a book of mine no matter what. They say I write them up and I hurt them. But that's not true."

"I remember," I said, "reading about Thomas Wolfe when his books came out. He was worried about the reaction in his hometown."

We eased across U.S. 23.

"Oh, it was terrible for him," Jesse Stuart said. "Couldn't go back home again. It was real bad for him all right."

"And you?" I said.

"I just went and wrote what came naturally to me," he said. "I'd write up a story as if it were true. I'd change names. I had to watch that. In *The Thread That Runs So True* I got out a map of Kentucky and went over all the names. I didn't allow any Kentucky name to be in that book. I called Greenup 'Blakesburg'—and there's no town named that in Kentucky. But this will throw you, Dick. Somebody in North Carolina wrote me a letter addressed to Blakesburg, Kentucky—and I got it! Did you ever hear tell of such a thing? But I try to keep real names of people out of my books."

"It's hard to gauge the vanity of readers," I said.

"You are right there," he agreed. He eased the car off the county road onto the W-Hollow road. A smidgin of black-top was all that was left of the paving. "There are some in that book that love being in it," he went on. "Then again, there are some that don't. . . ."

The hills closed in on us.

"Up there," he said, waving to the hill south of the road, "is seventy-four acres of the prettiest hilltop land you ever did see. I'm trying to give it to the county for a consolidated school. The school has to be within five miles of the county seat, and besides the site I'm offering free, the only other one is down by the river bottoms. They'll have septic tank prob-lems down there for sure. And they'll have to pay two thou-sand dollars an acre down there. I'm offering them seventy-four acres for one dollar, providing they don't name anything there for my family or me. Or my wife's family. But it's turned into a regular tug-of-war. I'm having the hardest time convincing them to take it!"

This bothered Jesse Stuart, too.

"Let me tell you something, Dick," he said. "If you live in a community and have a better house, even though you sweated hard to earn it with books and farming, some of the people will admire you, but some of the people won't. What I did here, anybody else could have done, but they didn't. I hardly ever had enough money ahead to buy additional pieces of land without borrowing. Only once or twice I did, but those were the exceptions. Why, some of them could have done it easier than I could have! An old man who used to drink beer with my dad down in Greenup would tell my dad, 'Mick, what about your boy going out there and buying up that old worthless land? It doesn't amount to anything.

It's old land. It's nothing!' And Dad would drink his beer and tell the man, 'I think Jesse is doing the right thing.' But don't you see? Any one of them could have done it, too."

The hills of W-Hollow surrounded us. On both sides of the road were the bits and pieces and patches of land Jesse Stuart had laboriously pieced together into a thing of beauty.

The poet rubbed his jaw and changed the subject. "A lot of people have to leave this area when it's ragweed season," he said. "But what gets me is the sycamore leaf. Put me next to a sycamore tree and I'll sneeze myself to death in summer. But mostly I'm sound. Oh, I went through the usual childhood diseases, but I had the best health. I never had a medical checkup back then. None of us country people did. But, boy, did I have good health and strength. Real endurance!"

"You didn't have a family doctor?"

"On rare occasions," he said. "But we had to be awful sick."

We turned up the fencerow that led to his home. We parked in front of his house. Jesse Stuart turned off the engine, then sat, thinking. Something was troubling him. As I waited I watched a butterfly poke among the meadow grass: a white dot in search of what?

"People," he said finally, "can't make a living in these hills any more." He continued his lonely requiem. "They're cut off from things. They just can't do it, Dick. They don't have the sales any more from the little crops the way they used to have. They don't dig enough coal, but the market for coal is shot anyway. And they won't leave. They don't want to give up their birthright." His gaze included W-Hollow—and *all* the lonely hollows in eastern Kentucky that man was passing by. "So they just sign up for government checks. They're

giving away their birthright for a government check, for
dole. Far out in the county, there's a lot of this going on.
Why, one man here in the hollow goes down and helps himself to the government commodities."

"Food stamps?"

"Yeah," said Jesse Stuart. "There are two in this vicinity
on 'em. Other places, the whole area is on 'em. It has become
a regular thing. I guess there are places in West Virginia
where everybody and his brother are on stamps."

We entered the house.

"What were you two discussing today?" Deane said. We
were, to her, two wet kittens lost in a rainstorm in need of
love. Her smile warmed us. The house was a sanctuary.

"Jesse Stuart, the legend," said the poet. Even to say the
word *legend* troubled him.

Deane nodded.

"How do you feel about it?" I asked Deane. "Here he is, a
legend. People make literary pilgrimages just to see the hollow and hope for a glimpse of him. Yet, he is also a man who
gets up every day, eats breakfast, and works. Does the legend
of him bother you, too?"

She shook her head. "No," she said. Her voice was soft. "I
don't think of him as a legend, Dick. I just can't think of him
at all that way. I've known him over the years, the years before we were married and the years after. To me, he's just
hard-working."

Jesse Stuart wandered into the other room to look over the
mail.

Deane went on speaking as if she had to say these things so
that I would love him, too.

"I know," she said, "there's always something troubling

him, bothering him—something he must do. If we're traveling, he has fun, he enjoys traveling, he sees everything, and he gets more out of traveling than anyone else I know. Yet, he's *recording* it. And it's always work. But a legend? No, oh, no. In the early days he was a farmer and we were barely surviving here. Was he a legend then? He was too busy to be a legend; he was doing things on the farm so we could eat. And as his books kept getting published and as we traveled and as he lectured, I began to see him in a different light. But a legend? I can't think of him as a legend, I guess. I think of him as my husband."

"And Greenup?" I said, remembering the eyes of the citizens as we had passed in Jesse Stuart's car. "How do they respond to him? Has their attitude changed?"

"No," said Deane. "I think they're a little more adjusted to us now, don't you, Jesse?" He had just reentered the room. "We don't have any close friends there," she added.

"I think they respect us," said the poet. "I don't know."

"We *are* liked and respected, Jesse," Deane said. Her voice was firm with reassurance. "We're accepted just as we are. We went to school there, Jesse. We graduated from high school there. We go to church there. We do our grocery shopping there and everything. We get our needs taken care of there."

"Together," said Jesse Stuart, "I guess we've taught half of Greenup. Half of it, I believe."

And Greenup? Which was the reality? The streets we visited or—

> *Winter has kept this town so oddly sleeping.*
> *Winter has made its face death-colored gray.*

Winter has kept its towering trees a-sleeping
And creeper vines now lifelessly a-creeping,
Winter has sent upon the pavements gray
Dead leaves to hither, thither, blow their way . . .

Jesse Stuart, the poet, memorized Greenup, but Greenup
—now sleeping beside U.S. 23,—never got around to
memorizing him.

THIRTEEN

<big>T</big>HIS is perfect up here," I said.

Jesse Stuart stood beside me, looking down into the hollow that contained—somewhere in the tangle of trees—all the home he would ever have.

"God, I *love* this country," he said.

We stood beside a fence where, many years before, coming to and from Greenup he had paused to jot down poetic oddments that later became *Man with a Bull-tongue Plow*. Hill-and-hollow people of yesteryear never followed roads to town because the roads were few. They took off, straight as the corn bird flies, nose pointed at their destinations and that was that: up hills, down steep grades, stepping over tangled roots and sudden mountain freshets—and pretty soon, wherever they were going, they got.

Jesse Stuart squinted into the sun and said:

"You see right through yonder, that little valley? And see that little round hill right next to her? Well, our daughter, when she was little, stood right here where we are now and she said, 'Daddy, it looks like a loaf of bread. It's bread loaf hill.' Well, we've called it Bread Loaf Hill ever since. . . ."

A mystic land, really. That's what I thought as I stood there. Jessica Jane Stuart had been born August 20, 1942.

214

That's not too far back as time goes. Yet, she grew up here where hills could still be discovered and still be given names by the children who discover them—and be of a time where the names would stick. She was of Now but she was, in part, of the generations of yesterdays that W-Hollow possessed. *She* had named a hill. Somehow that thought seemed beautiful to me. And there was Jesse Stuart, telling of the hill.

"There's been no fire on that hill, I've been told, in ninety-two years. Alf Ginnett told me that. The Ginnetts lived and grew up here. Why, for nearly a century there's been no fire on that hill. Timber has been cut off of it, they told me, about three times. Selective trees, you know. That's the way to cut timber: selective trees cut out. Today over there that timber is magnificent."

I looked around at the other hills, equally rich with timber.

"You've got some beautiful timber all over," I said.

He nodded.

"All over," he agreed. "But we've got the last big stand of it. A lot of people have come by here, looked at the timber, and wanted some."

"It must be frightening," I said, because it *had* to be said, "to know that someday somebody is going to come along and hack all this up."

He nodded again, still looking at the hill his daughter had named.

"They will if I don't do something," he said. "I don't believe my son-in-law will let them do this to this land. I know our daughter won't let them do it. But they're not of the hollow. They got their own things to do, haven't they? Neither one of them can take care of all of this." Reproach was not in

his voice, melancholy was. "There's no place for our daughter here. How in the world could she teach around this part?
Medieval Italian is what she's going after. As soon as she fin-
ishes a translation she will have her doctorate in it. Now
where in the world in eastern Kentucky can anybody teach
that? No place but the university. That's the only place I
know...."

"Her husband," he was saying, "is a graduate of Duke Law
School. He has finished seven years of school. He's got to
have a law college where he can teach. She'll be a teacher,
too. She can't keep out of it. It's in her blood. Oh, they'll
both be teaching somewhere. They're both real wonderful.
He's fine and so is she. They'll both end up teaching. Wait
and see."

But at a university far away.

That was the unsaid item.

After a moment, I said, "This valley, Jesse, will it last?"

He shrugged. To be a poet is to be a realist.

"I don't know," he said. He could only speak the truth.
"As long as my wife and I keep our health, it will. The
thought of later bothers me, Dick, but what can *I* do about
it? My son-in-law could come live here, but what could he
do? That wouldn't be fair for him. Our daughter Jane writes,
but she doesn't write enough, and teaching isn't enough to
keep the thousand acres going. Besides, they wouldn't know
how. Maybe a grandson, if I live long enough, will come
along and do it, but he would have to want to. It wouldn't be
fair to force." He looked around. "Where is there a better
place?" he said, but knew the answer; each has his own such
place.

To change the mood—a little—I said:

"How could you teach someone to love this place as you do?"

"You can't," he admitted. "But it's in Jane somewhere. She wouldn't let a single tree be cut. She'd be the kind, though, to have a university under all these trees, like the Greeks. Her academic background is Greek and Latin. But she would never destroy. I don't think she'd cut those meadows over there as much as the cattle chews away at them."

"Did she have a good childhood here?"

"A real good one," he said with pride.

"Did she go to school in Greenup?"

"She went as far as we could send her there," Jesse Stuart said. "But she had her problems. She was such a good student. They virtually attacked her there, you know."

"Because they were really attacking you?"

He looked at me carefully, then said a soft, "Yes, yes..."

We wandered in silence along the fence where once poetry had sprung to life. The morning sun was good. Flies and a few bees buzzed and swarmed. Cattle grazed, so we stepped carefully. The crickets—and the faint bark of a distant dog—were the only other sounds. Then, also in the distance, someone started to hammer: the slow methodical beat-beat-beat, then pause, there it went some more. Then it was gone. Silence land.

The poet felt almost compelled to talk of Jane. He summed her life up neatly: born in Ashland, August 20, 1942; wrote and published her first collection of poems, *A Year's Harvest*, 1957; student at American University in Cairo, Egypt, 1960–1961; student at University of Kentucky, Lexington, 1962–1963; taught Latin at Everglades School for Girls, Miami, Florida, 1962; married Julian Jurgensmeyer, 1963; received A.B. magna cum laude, Western Reserve University, Cleveland, 1964; teaching associate, department of classics, Indiana University, 1965–1967; summer student, Anglo-American Cultural Institute, Athens, Greece, 1966; M.A., Indiana University, majors in Greek and Latin, minor in Italian, 1967; birth of son Conrad Stuart, July 21, 1967; published *Eyes of the Mole*, 1967; traveled in France and Ethiopia, 1968; birth of son Erik, November 6, 1970.

But to the poet—and the father—these items were not his daughter.

We both leaned over the fence rail, looking absently into the valley, as he said:

"You know that one room off the living room? Well, that was hers and that was where she did her studying. She is one of the brightest girls I know. Only when she was studying, she resented anybody coming in there and bothering her. Maybe she didn't want to write because I was a writer. She wouldn't talk about it, but there she is, a writer now herself. You talk about someone who can handle a short story! She can do a beautiful short story. Why, when Ed Kuhn came to visit us he read some of her stuff and he said if she could have done a longer book, he would have taken her in a minute. But the book she had written was too short."

He watched a hawk circle, seemed preoccupied by that, but after a moment said:

"It was a story about mentals. Mentals have always fascinated Jane. You know, somebody a little screwy."

We continued our stroll along the fencerow.

"And I've seen her," he said, proud as fathers are, "get out and stagger out of the house, across the yard. She was forever exhausting herself with study. One day when she was going

out, taking the dog with her, I said, 'Jane, what's the matter?'
She said, 'Oh, Daddy, I don't know." I said, 'Well, you work
too hard. What have you just done in there?' She said, 'I've
just translated two hundred lines of Latin and one hundred
lines of Greek.' And I said, 'Have you done anything else?'
And she said, 'Yes. I've written seven poems.' So she took the
dog and went for a walk through the hollow. She came back,
fresh and straightened up and herself again. She was eighteen
or twenty at the time. There was no way to slow her down.
She couldn't help herself. She's been doing poems—well,
she's been doing them before she could put the words down.
Naomi Deane would put them down for her. She's been putting down words into poems since the time she could write.
And she's saved most of them."

And years later, her writing skills honed to perfection, she
would write of Aphrodite:

> *The virgin of the tides has powdered feet*
> *and slippery hands.*
> *She knows which way*
> *the wind will come*
> *down to the shore*
> *to lash away*
> *the uncut sand*
> *and shells still singing from the sun.*
> *She knows what sleeps*
> *beneath the sea*
> *and where the moon was made.*
> *She watched her own birth*
> *from a fragile stone*
> *that fell away under the steaming power*

of chiselling thumbs
and eyes that held a dream.

And Jesse Stuart, that sunny morning of the path of August, was saying to me:

"Dick, you ought to see a little book she did out here when she was twelve years old. She put all those poems together, entered them in the county fair, but didn't win anything. Well, I happened to show it to the man who edited *Land*, one of the old magazines. One of the greatest magazines, I swear, that ever came out of this country. Well, the editor saw her poems and he said, 'This is it.' His wife did the illustrations and the poems were published. They were published in book form in a little press he had in Maryland."

But another thought, saddening him, returned. A poet does not earn enough to keep a W-Hollow from those who would eventually hack away its timber.

A poem, however beautiful, would never save the trees. Time was running out.

August would soon be September—and then winter would be upon the land, perhaps for keeps.

Or, if there is an agony to spring, and there is, it is that spring exists.

By the time we reached his home on the hollow, the mail had arrived. Deane was sitting in the living room, sorting through it. She greeted us, then said with a voice both amiable and puzzled:

"I brought in the mail, Jesse, and opened some. I opened Jane's letter, but she evidently left out a page. It just doesn't make sense. . . ."

The poet spent ten minutes going through the mail himself, then joined his wife and me in the living room.

"Has Jesse told you about his driving?" Deane asked.

"No," I said.

But I *had* been aware of it. Jesse Stuart, the poet, is a well-edited creature. His driving is more casual. When touring the thousand acres—up, down, and sideways—of his W-Hollow land, he favors the Volkswagen station wagon, a dusty little blue car that seems to care less for roads than the poet himself does. Under the hand of Jesse Stuart, it skitters with bumpity-bumps along creek beds or across them, wobbles and wiggles along one-lane paths the cattle have created, and hums—as if pleased with itself—across smooth meadows. Jesse Stuart, like me, has yet to master the reverse gear in the VW. We both have the feeling it is *somewhere;* each time it proves to be somewhere else, and so we are never certain we are in reverse until we let out the clutch a little to see which way the car has decided to go.

Once, back in the steeper and more cavernous part of his land we decided to turn around. The road had been chiseled, it seemed, off the side of the hill. Out my window the view of the land was straight up. Out his side of the car, the view was straight down. Nonetheless, the little car, under his hand, was willing to make a Y, somehow, and head back the other way. He turned the wheel, the little car eased to the edge of the precipice, then hung there, awaiting his command. We were talking about something at the time—I forget what —but we were terribly involved. I know that. He found a gear he assumed to be reverse, we kept on talking, he let out the clutch, the car inched reluctantly forward to the brink, and neither of us worried. In a casual, everyday voice, Jesse Stuart said:

"I don't think I better go that way too far."

He found reverse eventually, we turned, and bounced back

along the road to the bottom of the valley. When I told my wife, Jean, of that moment, she paled. I have not told Deane of it. She will probably read it here. But I was not worried, nor was Jesse Stuart. I had faith in him and he had faith in his wonderful little car.

So when Deane had asked me if her husband had told me about his driving, I had answered truthfully. With *words*, he hadn't. Actually, he is an excellent driver, better than I am. His only weakness, I suggest, is locating the reverse gear on the VW—and this weakness, I suggest, is a universal one. I have the uneasy feeling that on each and every VW the reverse is in a different location. I also have the feeling that in any given VW the reverse will sometimes be here and sometimes be there.

"Well," said Deane, "Jesse didn't learn to drive until we had been married three years."

I accepted this.

"He learned to drive just before Jane was born," she added.

"I just got in the car and went," said Jesse Stuart, pride in his voice. "I went with her mother up to the hospital to see Naomi Deane."

"My mother couldn't drive either," said Deane.

"She sure couldn't," said Jesse Stuart.

"But mother said to Jesse, 'Jesse, you can do it. I'll watch the road and the stoplights and tell you when to stop,'" Deane related. "I almost had a heart attack when they walked into the hospital room together," she added.

"There wasn't much traffic," Jesse Stuart said, in his own defense.

Both still had searing recollections of the wreck that had

almost taken their lives, and the life of their unborn Jane, in a car Jesse wasn't driving.

"Did you ever think," I said, "that because of the wreck you might lose her?"

Deane's answer was quick and sure.

"No," she said. "I was always positive. Looking back, they were dark days. Perhaps we should have been more concerned, but we weren't."

"My mother worried," said Jesse Stuart.

"But I never did," said Deane simply.

"You were in a cast for a long time, weren't you?" I asked.

"Yes," she said.

"Two times," Jesse Stuart said.

"Well," she said, "I had the cast changed. We weren't sure I was pregnant at the time of the accident. We thought so, but we didn't know for a fact. And I had this back injury. . . ."

The Jesse Stuarts, traveling with another couple, were on their way to Mexico City, traveling through Mexico. They were driving the lonely land at night near Villa Amada. The driver wasn't driving fast. The empty road before them was dark and still wet from a heavy rain.

"And," said Jesse Stuart, "we saw this wolf cross the road. It was the only time in my life that I saw a wolf cross the road in front of a car. It was some kind of timber wolf."

A back tire blew.

"When a car goes over seven and a half times with women in it," said Jesse Stuart, his voice awed by the recollection, "seven and a half times . . ."

The poet and the driver had been thrown from the car but the two women had not.

"When I regained consciousness," said Deane, "I heard the radio playing and I smelled gasoline. It was dripping."

"The driver," said Jesse Stuart, "was knocked out with a concussion."

When the tire blew, the car hit the wet sand by the side of the road and started flipping, over and over and over, its doors opening, spilling the men, keeping the women.

"And some Indian came up," said Jesse Stuart. "He and I *lifted* that Chrysler up. You can't believe that, but we did. We lifted her up. And we got 'em out."

"The lady traveling with us had more severe injuries than I did," said Deane. "She was placed in a cast in El Paso and brought home by train in the cast. The doctor who saw me confirmed I was pregnant. He let me come home on the train, too, but Jesse had to lift me into the diner. When we got back home I was x-rayed immediately, and that's when they saw I had a twelfth dorsal fracture. So the doctor put me in a cast, too. They brought me home here where they'd put a hospital bed in the other room. Jesse's sister, Glynnis, who was having nurse's aide training, came to stay to take care of me. When the cast needed to be changed, we waited till the road out of the hollow was frozen so the ambulance could come in and get me. I went back to the hospital, had my cast changed, they changed my position, and I was in that cast about six months. I was in a walking brace until Jane was born."

"I saw the x-ray myself," said the poet, filled with cosmic curiosity. "This crushed dorsal. It was pinched down, like it had come out like a wedge. When they said it would come back, I couldn't believe it. How could nature put it back?"

"But it did," said Deane. "Calcium formed and rebuilt."

"And in the same pattern as the first," said Jesse Stuart. He was still amazed. "I checked this carefully. I had to see. I am interested in my wife," he added, the greatest understatement he made the whole time we were together.

"Well," said Deane, smiling at him, the smile seeming private, "many people were curious. There were stories, you know, wondering if I would ever walk again or would the child be normal."

"Did you have any doubts?" I said.

"No," she said.

"But don't you see," said Jesse Stuart to the world—to Deane, to me, to all the clocks that were ticking, to the meadow grass outside the window, to everyone—"under these circumstances, Jane was lucky to have been born. I don't know how she feels about life, but I think she loves it, too!"

We three digested this thought a moment.

Afterward, in a different voice, Jesse Stuart said, "You know, that's the only child we'll have. And look at what she is. I've told Naomi Deane, I've told everyone, and I don't care who hears me say it: we've got a million-dollar daughter! We *have*, too. Let's be frank about it. Look what a girl she is! We've seen 'em all, too, haven't we, Naomi Deane? We've seen among our friends, the bright ones and the dull ones. We've seen children in nearly every state in the Union and lots of foreign countries, and Jane is the best!"

"When she was born in August," I said, "the road back here wasn't in bad shape, was it?"

"No," said Deane. "There wasn't any bad weather. But it was on our minds, though. We were always thinking about getting out of here to the hospital. We just had to watch after a heavy rain. That would have been the worst. The car couldn't have made it till the roads dried off or drained. We'd have bogged in mud."

"Many a night," said Jesse Stuart, "I've walked along that road. In our younger days, me and Naomi Deane used to go to dances or somewhere. If the road was bad, we'd park the car and walk out and in."

"We'd drive as far as we could," Deane corrected.

"And the next day," said Jesse Stuart, "we'd get Uncle Jesse to get the mule team and pull the car out. Actually, we had one old mule that would do it. He'd just turn his head toward the barn and break us free, easy as pie. If he was heading to the barn, he'd just as soon uproot a tree as pull a car out of the mud. Boy, he was a powerful mule! And we'd sit in the car, driving, and out the mule would pull us!"

The poet paused to let a clock chime.

"Jane was a big girl when she was born," said Jesse Stuart.

"Around twenty-one inches long," said Deane.

"Something like that," said Jesse Stuart. "She was big."

"Did you have a girl's name picked out?" I said.

A moment's silence. Then, Jesse Stuart said, "No. Naomi Deane handled the girl. I would have handled the boy. I used to carry her in a basket everywhere. I would put Jane in a basket in that old Plymouth and I would look over at her even when I drove. I carried her around everywhere. If somebody didn't brag on her, I'd be insulted. Oh, me, what a child! I think she was a pretty baby. We had her in the hospital in Ashland. . . ."

Jesse Stuart had once written:

"Son," said my father, "take you a strong wife;
Take you a mountain girl strong as a tree—

It takes a tree to meet the winds of life.
Your Ma, she was the kind that suited me.
Get you a wife with eyes bright as a star
And teeth white as a thunder-cloud's white head;
Get one with cheeks red as the wild plums are
And ankles thin as runners on a sled.
And get yourself about six right pert sons
So they will carry on blood of their fathers;
And let them nurse from their mother's strong breasts;
Your six strong sons—maybe three strong daughters—
Raise them to be men in a world of men.
Let them take wives and multiply again."

"And Jesse," I said, "if you had a son what would he be like?"

The poet was quick to answer.

"Strong," he said. "I would teach him to use an axe and how to plow a straight furrow. He would be a powerful man, a football player maybe. . . ."

But the poet and his beautiful wife—her eyes "bright as a star," her cheeks "red as the wild plums are"—will have no son. Yet there is a balance. They have Jane—and Jane outweighs all the children that will never be. Jesse Stuart quickly admits he is a happy man. No one would disagree with this. No one at all.

Because, in honesty, how *dare* a man be lonely who can write:

I love to see corn bursting from the earth—
Three tender green blades growing in the sun.
I love to see the sown-cane bursting forth
And see bean sprouts with two half-beans on one.

I tell you then the call to earth comes back
And I cannot escape this deep-blood call—
Wheat in light waves—light-green—in thick waves black.
I watch wind waves of clover rise and fall
And walnut limbs wind-bent on shaded walk,
And here the whistling plowmen meet and talk—
They stand beside the wild raspberry stalks,
They speak of melons, sugar-corn and freezes,
Of sultry days and cool summer breezes—
The voice of Spring will always call them back. . .

But, as I sat and talked with Jesse Stuart and his wife when the conversation had been of Jane, I heard words they didn't say as well as the words they said.

I heard the winding down of W-Hollow.

"What's your next project here?" I said.

"Just to keep the place running," Jesse Stuart said. "It's reached an apex. I don't want any more land, except maybe I'd like to have the upper side of one pasture to straighten it out a little."

"Other than that," I said, "you're through?"

"You bought more tile," Deane said. "You'll have to get it brought home. Remember?"

"Yes," said the poet almost absently. "Now where was it I bought that?"

"When Bud gets his hay cut," said Deane, "and when he gets the tobacco in, he'll bring in the tile and put it somewhere." She looked at me and smiled. "We always have something going," she said. "But no more big projects," she added.

Jesse Stuart peered at me, but I could not—did not try to—read his look.

"I used to never stop projecting," he said. "Like so many trees set a year. I'm still planning books, though. I've got two coming out in seventy-one. I had two published this year. By seventy-two I hope to have two more."

"You're always finding some of his writing?" I asked Deane.

"Yes," she said. "We find it, just all around."

"But there are no magazines anymore," said Jesse Stuart. "The magazine market is gone."

"And the book market?" I said.

"I'm afraid that is going, too," said Deane.

"I've gone through old magazines," said Jesse Stuart, "for names to find out how many writers who started with me haven't been heard from anymore. Some died. In the fifties some drifted away. A few were holding in the sixties. Only here we are in the seventies—and I seem to be the only one left. Well, there is Bill Saroyan. . . ."

We paused again as another clock chimed another hour. For us that August morning it was the last hour.

We had run out of words.

We had said it all.

About the Author

THE working life of Cincinnati-born Dick Perry has kept both monotony and the wolf from the door. Once a turntable operator at the railroad roundhouse in his home town, he was urged by the New York Central to accept early retirement because "engines kept missing the table and falling into the pit." He moved on to radio announcing for small-town stations in the Midwest; turned to a variety of radio and TV writing and production jobs for networks and agencies; covered lost dogs and the police things for the *Cincinnati Post*. Bewildered with all these areas of commerce and industry, he became a free-lance writer of plays, books and short stories several years ago. Married and the father of three teenagers, he now lives and works in Oxford, Ohio.

REFLECTIONS OF JESSE STUART

On a Land of Many Moods

by Dick Perry

Jesse Stuart—novelist, poet, magazine author, writer of nonfiction, lecturer, a living legend among Southern writers—participates here in a bold experiment. Trusting the man who visited him for eight days to talk about his 1000-acre farm, his writing, his views on the world today, he spoke freely to Dick Perry about the things closest to his heart.

As Stuart himself says, "What wouldn't I have given to be able to have such a record, made in their lifetimes, of the writers I have admired most—Mark Twain, Robert Frost, Edgar Lee Masters, Carl Sandburg . . ."

A man who cherishes his privacy here invites you into his home to talk about what means most to him—his wife, his daughter, his land, his work, his childhood, his friends, the future of an America whose ecology is imperiled by thoughtless and selfish men.

You will agree with some of Jesse Stuart's opinions and disagree with others, but you will, wherever you stand, admire the courage it took to let the world know where *he* stands on controversial issues of the '70s. "Run, sheep, run" was never Mr. Stuart's game.

Author Dick Perry has caught all of this for you to see. He is a long-time admirer of Jesse Stuart's work, but no more inclined to agree with all of his opinions than any other author who is his own man. Cincinnati-born Perry's working life has kept both monotony and the wolf from the door. Once a turntable operator at the railroad

(continued on back flap)